M000189571

INUA ELLAMS: PLAYS ONE

Inua Ellams

# PLAYS ONE

OBERON BOOKS
LONDON

WWW.OBERONBOOKS.COM

First published in 2019 by Oberon Books Ltd
521 Caledonian Road, London N7 9RH
Tel: +44 (0) 20 7607 3637 / Fax: +44 (0) 20 7607 3629
e-mail: info@oberonbooks.com
www.oberonbooks.com

*The 14th Tale* © Inua Ellams, 2009;
*Untitled* © Inua Ellams, 2010;
*Knight Watch* © Inua Ellams, 2012;
*Black T-Shirt Collection* © Inua Ellams, 2012.

Inua Ellams is hereby identified as author of these plays in accordance with Section 77 of the Copyright, Designs and Patents Act 1988. The author has asserted his moral rights.

All rights whatsoever in this play are strictly reserved and application for performance etc. should be made before commencement of rehearsal to The Agency, 24 Pottery Lane, Holland Park, London W11 4LZ (info@theagency.co.uk). No performance may be given unless a licence has been obtained, and no alterations may be made in the title or the text of the play without the author's prior written consent.

You may not copy, store, distribute, transmit, reproduce or otherwise make available this publication (or any part of it) in any form, or binding or by any means (print, electronic, digital, optical, mechanical, photocopying, recording or otherwise), without the prior written permission of the publisher.

A catalogue record for this book is available from the British Library.

PB ISBN: 9781786828200
E ISBN: 9781786828200

Cover image: Inua Ellams

Printed and bound by 4EDGE Limited, Hockley, Essex, UK.
eBook conversion by Lapiz Digital Services, India.

Visit www.oberonbooks.com to read more about all our books and to buy them. You will also find features, author interviews and news of any author events, and you can sign up for e-newsletters and be the first to hear about our new releases.

Printed on FSC® accredited paper

10 9 8 7 6 5 4 3 2 1

# Contents

# THE 14<sup>TH</sup> TALE

*The 14th Tale* was first performed at Battersea Arts Centre on 31st of July 2008 performed by Inua Ellams.

*Directed by* Thierry Lawson
*Lighting by* Michael Nabarro

The play is set in a hospital waiting room and is told with flashbacks. The stage is sparse save for a chair on the far right corner. The performer wears a t-shirt and trousers splattered round the torso and pocket with red liquid giving the impression of blood.

# Part 1 //

## // HOSPITAL

The light that limps across the hospital floor
is as tired as I feel; it is the pale green of nausea
the shade that rises slowly, pushes upwards
and out. I want to burst, out, through, past
the sliding doors to the windy wet night, wind
my way to the kind of corners I am used to,
the kind of troubles I know and climb my way
out. But I still myself, swallow till the light
shallows, count five, four, three, two, one…

/ x /

I'm from a long line of trouble makers.
Of ash-skinned Africans, born with clenched fists
and a natural thirst for battle, only quenched
by breast milk. They'd suckle as if the white silk sliding
between gums were liquid peace treaties written

from mums. Their small thumbs would dimple
the soft mounds of brown flesh, goose-pimple chests
till the ceasefire of sleep would creep into eyes,
they'd keep till the moon set and wake twice hungry,
twice vexed, raring to go. My grandfather, six years old,
tough and scatterbrained as all boys would be, once
in a gathering of tribes, crawled under tables past
the feet of tribal chiefs, surfaced by the serving dishes
cupped his hands together, began shovelling
the special treat of fried moose meat into his mouth.

When the cry of *'thief! thief!'* rang out, he turned,
wondering who had such audacity – to find an angry
line of village cooks coming his way. With his face
still stained with the spiced juice of diced moose,
he grabbed another handful and fled into the dark
woods chased by siblings, pets and abuse.

They say he ran so fast, the ground gasped, forgot
to take footprints; they lost him in the fields.
But the story never left memory, was told around
campfires and followed his son (my father)

to secondary school where a campus-wide trend
of long nicknames was maximised by a senior boy
who thumbed through a textbook's index,
added *Periplaneta Americana,* the most elaborate
he could find, to *Nevada* his old title and swaggered
through halls slapping younger boys
for mispronouncing the name.


Once, from a crowd gathered at lunch, *Periplaneta
Americana Nevada* struck six boys till father,
rebelling against seniority, revealed the title
was Latin for desert cockroach! The crowd laughed
as *Nevada* chased my father who tripped him
through a thorn bush and the long line of trouble
makers meets me: inheritor of fast feet and father's
contempt for authority, who, try as I might
to break the line, have battled adults, been chased
through schools and have climbed out more windows
than burglars do. I wonder which story will reach
my son and wonder more what he will do.


/ x /

7

It started in the hot dusty clay streets of Plateau State,
Nigeria. They say I successfully conned the doctors into
thinking I was the only one; my first trick was hiding
my twin sister for eight months and two weeks till
the shoddy equipment finally picked up her heartbeat:
I climbed into the world already in trouble!


By seven, I was a small, sweet-smiled pretty boy
who terrorised lizards lazing under constant suns,
had a confidence that conspired to get me caned
least once a day. But I escape one Sunday, when
the church choirs out *In the name of Jesus, in the
name of Jesus, I have a victory…* Their voices rise
like glorified sound clouds, filter through the daylight
-dyed halls to the Sunday school back-room stifled
with kids, filter to the teachers who hum along
before asking:

*Oya, Oya children, did you do your homework?
Did you read the chapter that I asked you to?
Did you read your Bible? Oya, Inua, go to the front
of the class and tell us how Moses got water from the Rock.*

I hadn't done the work: between *Home Alone* reruns,
tournaments of table soccer, chasing lizards and teaching
the neighbour's dog new tricks, I hadn't touched a Bible
that week, so I slouched to the front of the class
thinking wildly and chose to improvise...


*Ahh teacher you know… Eh, Moses got water from the tap.*

*Is that so Inua?*

*Yes Aunty, where else?*

*How is that possible eh? When there weren't any pipes?*

*Erm… he … he had an elephant! …*

> Searching frantic for something, anything to help,
> I spied a small piece of clockwork glinting
> on the classroom floor. I picked it up and inspiration,
> like a white light blazed across my mind. I bit my lip
> and went with it…

*erm... yes, he had an elephant -underground- and he carved an*
*intricate system of clockworks, of cogs and wheels and vices around the*
*Elephant. Yes, and when he turned the tap, it turned the cogs, turned*
*the wheels and tightened the vices around the Elephant's brokotus and*
*he trumpeted out in pain, pushing water through his trunk, through the*
*tap and into the ground ! Yes... er... no? no?*
*A-ah, Aunty, Teacher! What did I do?*


*Stupid boy, how dare you! That is blasphemy you hear me? You are*
*blaspheming, that is three strokes, gimme your hand jare...*


She flexed her muscles, swiping wildly with canes,
these were long flexible raffia sticks, polished till
they glinted as if lined with metal. Trying to put
as much distance between me and crazed teachers,
I dashed down the middle of the class, barrelled
through the doorway, down the halls, out
to the dusty courtyard with the nuns in hot pursuit,
jumped into the tallest tree and climbed my way up
leaving the hurricane of nuns below, praying
and cursing me.

They called my father. I was too high to hear voices,
but after a minute's speak, their arms waving
frantically, they turned, leaving Dad who asked me
down. We left the compound and walked the dusty road
home in silence till he asked what happened. I told him
the story. After trying not to, but finally bursting out
in belly laughs, it quietened to a silence shuffled only
by my feet dragging the dry road home. Nervously
I asked him, *Daddy, am I in trouble, will I be punished?*

*No, it is too early for that to work eh, besides there is a vague order to
things, things happen when they are meant to, don't worry, your time
will come. Your time will come.*

## Part 2 //

His name was Johnny Bassey.
His name was Johnny Bassey.


Of all the troubles I have been, of those I've left
frustrated or crying, most deserving of all was he.
If ever we meet, I hope he'll have forgotten; I've
never caused anyone such pain since. In a boarding
school in Nigeria, it is a dark afternoon, mid-wet
season, all the world is grey. The torrent of rain
is a vertical river current cascading from the clouds
 – all the colours dulled as though surrendered
to the storm. The trees and buildings weighted
by the water are tired, battered and drowned.
All that is alive, all that is vibrant is the chant
of *fight! fight! fight!* rising from a circle of boys,
their voices communions to gods of war, fists
pounding the air. *fight! fight!* I'm at the centre
with Jebo – my best friend – as Johnny Bassey,
the head boy eggs him on…

*Jebo beat that boy! Hit him, punch him if not I'll flog you tonight! You hear me? No Jebo Inua, beat this boy right here! fight! fight!*

> I try to rise above their cries, look Jebo in his eyes
> and say,

*Jebo don't listen to them there's no reason for us to fight for his entertainment. Listen, if he flogs you, he'll flog me too eh? We'll both be beaten, Jebo are you hearing me?*

> But Jebo is frightened, has the wild look
> of a rabbit caught in lamplights, Jebo comes forward
> swinging, I back away till I'm pressed against
> Johnny Bassey who pushes me towards Jebo's fists,
> Jebo hits me in the chest. I try to speak, try to cover
> my face, fend off blows and resist retaliating,
> but Jebo swings till my lips bleed, swings till I fall
> to the floor, swings and comes more. Somewhere
> a voice warns of a teacher coming. The circle
> dissipates leaving Jebo who grabs me by my shirt
> and pulls me up as I notice a dampness in his eyes…

*Inua are you okay? Are you bleeding? Ah! You're bleeding! I'm really sorry, I did not mean to punch you so hard eh Inua are you okay?...*

*Jebo, don't touch me jor, how could you beat me eh? I'm your best friend! I was talking to you!*

*Sorry Inua eh, but you know he beat me last week for the same thing, I couldn't let it happen again, I still have the bruises, sorry eh?*

*Don't touch me Jebo, go away, I don't want to see your face eh? Just go away... Jebo are you crying? Ah, it is okay, oh! I am fine, stop crying. But we have to get him back Jebo! We have to get Johnny Bassey back!*

*Wait...*

*What are you doing tonight?*

// Sound: Night. Countryside.

/

When the sun fell, night settled on the campus
and the only lights were pinpricks of fire flies
dancing in the still damp darkness. I called Jebo
and two close friends. Together we crept, filling

the shadows with the dark intention of ourselves,
sticking as thin as silence to the sides of the hostel
buildings, our heartbeats bursting with adrenaline,
we snaked our way to the senior's dorm.


There were four of us: one left as the look-out outside
one inside by the window I climb through, with Jebo
– his eyes focused and keen and me with a tube
of toothpaste, *MacCleans*, bent over Johnny Bassey's
 sleeping form... Quietly, peeling back the covers,
I squeeze a thick line onto the bottom of his shirt and
press it into the fabric, squeeze a line onto each wrist,
a thick line onto the cuffs of each sleeve, thick lines
across both knuckles, lastly a line under his lower
closed eyelids, drop the finishing touches to the floor,
tickle his feet till he stirs and scarper into the dark,
stealing across the hostel grounds to the bushes.
Huddled in the fields close to the building,
we wait for it to begin.

We imagine it all: The first tingle, the cold burning
sensation, the chill that will climb up his lower eyelids,
the slow waking from dreams, the absent minded

wiping with knuckles adding to the paste, how
he'd flip his wrists, rub harder, faster, adding more,
how he'd panic, reach for cuffs, find no clean cloth,
no relief, just more pain, lift his shirt to eyes,
find no way out, roll off his bed to a floor stacked
with thumbtacks, how he'd hop!

We imagined his loud shallow cries running
to the bathroom, we laughed ourselves stupid
in the bushes trying to keep hushed. But when
the scream came, so insane was our laughter,
we crashed out the bushes, collapsed in a
bundle of tears and limp limbs: a mud covered
quartet cackling into the night, laughed so loudly…

We were caught! Punished! In front of the entire
school, whipped ten strokes each and one extra
for laughing as Bassey hopped in, feet wrapped
in, patterned with polka-dots of blood,
also given a plot of elephant grassland the size
of two classes to clear with a cutlass. All things
considered, we got off lightly and as we trooped
out to the fields, still in high spirits, Jebo half-

wrestled for my cutlass saying he felt guilty,
wanted to clear my patch for me. I fought back:


*Jebo, leave it alone, Jebo, it's okay eh? that's what friends are
for, Jebo it's fine.*


// Hospital


Can I see him now?… What do you mean *No,* I've
been waiting for half an hour!… Is he okay?… Is
there anything you can tell me?… THERE MUST
BE SOMETHING!… Okay, I'm calm! I'm calm…
Pardon?… Erm My clothes? Oh, don't worry… I'm
sorry… It's just… you know… Yes a cup of water
will be fine… listen, I'm really sorry about… you
know. If anything, anything at all, I'll be right here...
thanks.

## // Part 3

Twelve years old and I've mastered the art
of boarding school, I'm a Pro. Been punished
so much, my hands no longer blister from cutlasses
besides I've forged doctors letters declaring
I'm allergic to grass, dust and asthmatic. Pretty
useless, I'm punished to fetch endless buckets
of water but I'm working on that, I Am Working
On That! I know to sweet talk the dinner ladies
for firewood, distract them long enough for Jebo
to steal armfuls of plantains, know how to gather
stones, build campfires and roast them when
the months cold, I said it I'm a Pro. I know how
to pad my backside with text books and t-shirts
to take the pain when canes blow — I'm a Pro.


July '96, I get a phone call from home, Daddy has
a promotion, we have to leave for London, England.
Do we return? Unknown. And I cry with Jebo.
Tears hurt harder than blisters, cutlasses toothpaste,
and raffia stick, I cry all the way home, all the way
through packing, through flying, I sulk through

Heathrow Airport, through the first day of school.
Through the culture shock, through the first time
I'm called a *nig nog...* I only stop when I ask
the boy beside me:


*Eh, Garri. Gaaaaryyy. Gary, where's the teacher's cane?*


*What?*


*Gary you know? The teacher's cane? Is it made of raffia? I can handle
that one!*


*What?*


*Gary, don't you speak English?*


*Listen mate, I am bloody English and I 'eard you da first time bruv,
but teachers don't beat students bruv, dat's 'llegal, ya get me, das
'llegal!... Wait... You mean they beat you back in Africa? Liberties!
Bruv! Liberties! Don't take that! That's deep! Liberties!*

*Shhhh Gary? Shhhh, Wait, are you saying the teachers don't have canes?*
*The teachers don't have canes...*

For two weeks, I go insane, I forget to walk – run
everywhere... this half-boy, half-blur, Nigerian thick-
accented black attack, scattering down halls. I jump,
glide and slide past teachers, arrive three minutes late
for each lesson, wait till the class quietens, just to burst
open doors, pause till all eyes are on me, grab
my balls and say: *ahh, just checking!*


Grandfather's feet and father's contempt for authority
catapult me across the swirling new world. I learn
new swear words, that this (masturbation) is universal,
that Mel B is the finest Spice Girl and if you spray Lynx
on a patch of fabric and breathe deeply, there's a ringing
in your ears and you giggle like little girls. Eventually,
the novelty wears, teachers see past my practised blank
stares, my African accent thins and a new boy joins
the class, far more interesting... His name is Luis.


Dad said things happen when they are meant to,
that there's a vague order to things... from how dust

clusters to sand particles; hardens to diamond rings,
to star alignments... from how a moose meat thief
offsprings me to how a pendulum swings; how we
read such signs shape our world and beings.

His name is Luis. He is different from me. His eyes
are thin slits with pebbles of tar for pupils, his hair
comprises of long light wisps that spill into the air
about him, his skin is the palest I've seen.
He is Chinese, doesn't speak much English, calls
his mother tongue mandarin, between you and me,
I don't like him. But mother taught me better,
so I still my tongue, smile when he tries to talk
and tag along towing this resentment.

It's the brief between humanities and maths lesson.
We know Mr Randel is off sick. Supply teachers,
all spawned from the land of useless, won't notice
four boys gone from a class of thirty so we feign
we're thirsty, ask to go back to the fountain, duck
into the boys bathroom, lift the cracked window
till it's sized enough to squeeze through and hang–

drop to the sunny outside by the bike sheds. There
is Jack, Daniel, Luis and Me. The ground is a mosaic
of decayed leaves, splashed bird droppings and
cigarette butts. None of us smoke: we spend the first
few minutes getting over the fear of being caught,
then we begin to talk.


Now, we don't speak of video games, cars, girls or films
– the usual topics the minds of boys skim, instead
with voices high, pitched in excited tones, we speak
of excrement. Shit. In such detail do our tongues roam.
We speak of the floaters, the sleepers, small pellets
that seem to ricochet out, the mammoth ones, and tough
number twos that seem to fight back! Jack mimes
facial expressions, pushes and strains till his skin stains
red, Daniel makes the sound effects, I *phew* and *whew*
the redder Jack gets and Luis who vaguely understands
begins to laugh. And perhaps all this talk summons
the forces of nature for five minutes later, it gets real.


We line up against the school walls
with an uncontrollable urge and begin to pee.

Luis catches on and joins as our hips snake and
spell our names...

*I.N.U.A. Luis... Luis... wait for the fullstop.*

*Plop!*

Now, whenever I pee, just before the custom to stretch,
shake and ensure there are no drops left, I get this
funny sensation you know. It begins as a tickle, a soft
stroke between my shoulder blades, slows down my
spine, gathers momentum and explodes in a ticklish
uncontrolled spasm. I've known this for as long as
I've known time. Of the four boys who passed urine,
only one spasmed as I and turning, found surprising
to my eyes, Luis to share this shudder, my spine. And
here is where the vague order to things come, where
how we read such signs change our world and beings...
this is no star alignment, no pendulum swing, but
finding Luis to share this shudder, my spine sparked a
new way of thinking.

Since then, I've looked on all strange men as possible
brothers in spine. That regardless of race age, colour

creed, brotherhood is an undiscovered shudder away.
So excited am I, my accent blacks back to African,
I babble incoherently to

*Luis, don't you get it, my spine tingles, Your spine tingles, tingling spine…*

Through the thick of Mandarin he gets it. He gets it
and draped over each other, we laugh as if we sniffed
a can of Lynx each. Jack and Daniel don't get it. I try
to explain through stomach cramps and Luis arms,
when a passing girl hears the havoc of our voices, turns
the corner sees us and runs to get a teacher. We grab
bags and jackets, get ready to run… then realise our
names are wet, dripping, written on the school walls.
Caught, we're punished for skipping class and defiling
school property. As for the girl, I get her back!

Night fall finds me home. Through mouthfuls
of jollof rice, I tell Dad about Luis's spine
and vengeance. Dad laughs, reminds:

*Listen oh, you must grow out of this someday.*

Then adds,

*Okay, your time will come, just don't get caught.*

> The plan is simple. Her name is Stacey Flood.
> She is as wide as she is tall. Wears too tight Levis
> 501s that funnel past her waist when she sits.
> If you're unfortunate to catch a glimpse, you'll see
> a flat mashed freckle-speckled-chicken-raw ass
> the size of the grand canyon staring back.
> I wait patient as a rock face till she snoozes
> in the dinner hall like she usually does, creep
> towards her flanked by Jack and Luis…

*Shhhhs! Get back! You'll wake her! Shhhushs*

> Slowly I take out a package wrapped in kitchen foil
> that I sweet talked the dinner ladies into leaving
> in the freezer, ease back the silver sheet, prise apart
> two ice-cubes: between sits a cold frozen 5p coin.

29

I dangle it over Stacy's soft cheeks, line it with
the cavern of her grand canyon, where her butt
splits…and let it go…

*Ahhhhh!!!!*

*Luis did you see that? Jack we got her back! That was priceless!*

// Hospital

I can see him now?… Thanks, thank you so much…
Okay Inua, breathe, four, three, two, one… Hello,
hey… I'm good thanks. You?… Pardon? No, this…
don't worry about it… So what are the doctors
saying?… A what?… In your BRAIN!?… You
may never… No?… It's too soon…What? What do
you mean visiting hours are over? Okay, five more
minutes… They have to runs tests. They couldn't
possibly know that yet… Mm hmmm… yes but…
Pardon? Just two more minutes! Just… damn! Okay…
Okay. I'll see you tomorrow… first thing… Okay?…
Bye… bye.

They say he may never walk again.

## Part 4 //

Mid-teens we moved to Dublin, to a world more
alien than London was, a world so far from Nigeria,
I was the only black boy in school! First break time,
the attempt to blend in didn't work. Feeling like
a weed in the gnarled garden of Ireland's green,
a reluctant ambassador for Africa, I spruced up
my image, tried to stay clean, but still trouble came…

There was the parent's evening when, commenting
on mothers walking past, I spotted a thin-waisted
red-headed Celtic dazzler drifting across the car park,
nudged the boys, said…

*Oi, would yous look at that ride!*

The guys on the left collapsed in hysterics whilst
a deathly silence owned the right, I turned
to catch Ross Lynch, star rugby player, an inch
from my face say

*That's My Mother!*

Ross hunted me for three days straight, stalked me
through the emerald/grey maze of school. I evaded
capture with Grandfathers's feet, but was too slow
for that Friday by the gates when, after waving
goodbye to friends, I didn't hear the

*WATCH OUT!*

till it was too late, everyone scattered, Ross rode
into me on his moped, engine snarling, spitting
fire, front wheel cannoned into my chest, back-
wheel spun over my pelvis, I staggered home
with skid marks on my crotch!

There was the Saturday night we invaded school,
fashioned hoops from dustbins, played basketball
on the rooftop. I learnt the hard way – life doesn't flash
past when death threatens. Four points into the game,
police sirens sliced the night. We scrambled low
over the rooftops, tried to hang-drop off the three-
storey building when the brick I tightly gripped came

Basketba

loose. Slipping into the black nothingness, the fatality
of a fall screamed through me till Ross (now the good
friend) grabbed my hands and hauled me up.
I trembled as we ran across the green, dodging
police torch lights like laser beams.


I left the garden of Ireland singed with a Celtic fire
and a mishmashed accent of the straight speak
of Africans, stiff lip cockney and the thrust
of Southern Dublin, arrived in London more
scatterbrained than ever!


/ x /


Time passed tumultuous, trouble flared, but in feline
form where even the weather, famed for disrupting
the transport system; the inch of rain which would
stay workers away, even a freak winter cold or
the now often blizzards, or night-reports that warned
*Stay indoors, don't stray from home,* even that couldn't
hold me back from six months with Ella, whose chin

was porcelain-perfect with four freckles like dust
speckles I'd tickle till she laughed, or five months
with Anna, finest nose from Southern France, au pair,
from Brockwell who danced to deep trance, or four
months with Paris, ex Parisian/Persian queen! Whose
skin glowed golden and tinged a touch olive, or nine
months with Boden, feisty hockey player, always
bruised from head to toe, save the small of her back
which would flutter if you touched it like loose tissues
stacked against breeze; even gale force never held
me back, scatterbrained, I'd hack across city, cross
town until one stopped me frozen, dead in my tracks.


Her name was Donna Lorde and she had lashes
that lazed the world. Hair that cascaded crazily, locks
that kept me captive. I did not seek freedom, wanted
to stay captivated by long looks and her flowing mane
of wild stallions, formed of powder puffs and pouts,
she was gorgeous. We met on a night ordained by
the ordinary. The stars reflected in the window pane
dribbled mere suggestions of light that mingled with
the rain. I told her that I would like to see her again
and lip-printed her left cheek. A week later, sheltered

from London's lazy rain, we first-kissed, our tongues
like dancers, lips the dance-floor, heart beating
the backing track to tongue tip tango, kissing as though
Shango flung small sweetened lightening bolts
between us like firework-flavoured mangoes…
In this fruit frenzy and lightening shift, she tells me
she does not do relationships. That should have sent
alarm bells ringing but I was caught between wild
stallions and electric mangoes. All I remembered
was a comma in a cascading kiss… besides, no-strings
-attached loving was a luxury I could not miss, so I'm
like:

*Yeah, that's what I'm talking about!*

Three weeks later, I know her mind to be greater
than her fine body's form, I want to be the duvet
that keeps her warm, to be there when brain waves
collide so I can ride its after surf till the morning
comes. She senses this change in me, reminds me
she does not do relationships, I reply

But harbouring fugitive fantasies of us with entwined
shadows, I did not want to let go: It started with me
holding on long after we'd stop kissing, with waking
up at night to watch her chest rising, and falling and
perspiring forehead glisten, with whispering her first
name with my surname just making sure it fits.


She, sensing this changing growing started un-sowing
those lightning seeds till our bouts became sparse
forays where my heart showing caused her to freeze.
I tried giving her space to breathe, that a graceful
absence might make her see that though laced
with thoughts of lengthening light seeds, this could still
be easy… Till she tells me this has gone too far, has
pushed past friendship to something greater. That type
of feast she just cannot cater. She stays away for a week.

/ x /

I go round unannounced with a bouquet of rose
flowers: my hopes and dreams soft and tainted as
the fragrance in my arms, reach to push the doorbell
and hear laughter waft from the second floor window,
step back, peek, I see another man, head thrown back,
her face delicately pressed to his, her hair cascades
softly, she whispers to him, voice tickling his throat…
And all I see is black, all I taste is venom, all I feel
is anger, the dark fired kind, such rage, such rage,
I shred the roses to pieces, thorns tear into my hands,
palms bleed. I pace in the opposite side of the street,
think black, think venom, think fire, think and plot,
think and plot till he leaves. Then inspired by blood
and roses disappear for an hour, return under the cover
of dusk with pockets filled.

I cross over to stand in the shadows of the tree
that punches through the pavement, grows up
beside her open bathroom window. It is night
and there's venom in my eyes. I climb up, inch
my way through the rough foliage of trees, leaves
rustle like a thousand nuns' voices asking me down
I crush their stems like throats, climb up till I'm lined
with the bathroom window, stretch, grab, pull

and arch myself over, through and land softly
on the bath mat.


It is so quiet, the moonlight bouncing round the room
makes noise. It licks the tiled walls, tooth brushes,
towels and the shower curtain I draw back, reach,
pluck the shower head from its hold, gently unscrew
the metal cap. Taking from my pocket two jumbo-sized
tubes of red acrylic paint, I squeeze till the tubes
are flat and emptied into the shower head and try
to screw the metal cap back on. With each twist
it squeaks but in the death silence of the night
it sounds like tombstone dragged against stone,
I slow down, twist, twist twist…


// Sound of phone ringing.


*Hello? Hi… Hi… listen Sis, this is not a good time. I
can't talk right now…Erm Hi Donna! Calm down, stop
screaming! It is Inua, It's just me… Sis, I'm kinda busy, just
in the middle of something… Donna, don't call the police!*

*You'll wake the neighbours, It's not a good idea!...*
*Listen Sis, I'm in the middle of something, just*
*call me back... Hello?... What?... Donna shhhshs!...*
*Hospital? I'm coming... Donna sorry, I have to go...*

# Part 5 //

Time freezes in the hospital ward.
The doctor's words gather about me and tower
till a shadow – dark as uncertainty – falls tangling
everything. Rooted in the hospital ward,
for the first time, ever, I am frozen, I am still.
This is beyond trouble. There is no authority
to contempt, no walls, no teachers… no…


My father had a stroke. A blood vessel burst
bleeding into the right side of his brain, cutting
signals to the left side of his body. The muscles
there are stiff, only half his face moves, his speech
is slurred, he cannot walk. He rolls off his bed
when he sleeps so has to be strapped in with
a tangle of white tubes and wires. A nightmare
of machines and monitors bleep, flash in random
patterns – a mayhem of lights and life flickering.

Boys should never see their fathers fall.
It upturns worlds and steals words. No longer
thorn of authority, living legacy of troublemakers,
overnight, Dad becomes just a man. And I his son,
mortal – unable to run.


Weeks pass in the hospital ward. I watch Dad drift
in and out of consciousness till one Friday the sun
spills a half-light that ghosts over hunched shoulders
into my cupped palms. I hold a Bible and read Dad
psalms, but my tears blur the letters. I read in
stuttered staccato that wakes Dad from sleep.
Drowsily he peeks from the folds of hospital clothes,
catches me and the Bible both dripping tears.
In short slurred words, he asks why I cry
and I want to tell him why. How it is too soon
for him to go. How suddenly I feel disconnected
from the line, alone as a barefooted child walking
a dusty road home in silence, asking the world
*Why*? Instead I say


*I don't know.*

And he laughs. Because he's seen it all before, says

*There is a vague order to things… things happen for a reason. Don't*
*worry, I'll be fine. Maybe… time has come eh?*

and I accept this. I let it wash over, let it come…
And slowly, things begin to unravel; a vague order
begins to rise. Uncles and aunts call with demands
and questions… My instant contempt for authority
falls as I note the motives, the fear in their words.
Dad comes home, I master how to tiptoe. Evenings,
go for walks, speed has to be controlled. I slow down
as Dad learns to walk again. Broken brain wires spark
and form again. We talk of the past, tempt the future,
litter it with song, tickle it with laughter…

They say when death laughs at a man, all a man
can do is laugh back. We work by lamplight.
Dad writes a letter. I research how stroke victims
are prone to second ones, when the lamp dies.
He reaches out into the death-defined darkness,
unscrews the light bulb, delicate in his back-to
-nimble left hand, and laughs.

In the darkness, my chest swells like a sunrise,
such light, it bleaches the living room, breaches
the dusk, reaches back and stops time for the souls
of trouble makers who form a vague line, Dad
beckoning that I take my place in front of these
ash-skinned-Africans, born with clenched fists
and a natural thirst for battle, only quenched
by breast milk.

I've battled adults, been chased through schools, have
climbed out more windows than burglars do. Finally,
through the vague order of these things, my time has
come like Dad said it would. I wonder when this story
will reach my son and wonder more what he will do.


END.

UNTITLED

*To name something is to call it into life, to determine its future. If we let our children name themselves, will they author their own destinies? Will the nameless ones be free?*

# Introduction

## THE INGREDIENTS:

1) I have a twin sister. When we were 3, I cried like a lost child the first day of separation at nursery. She didn't even look back. I changed quickly and as we grew and met other twins, I wondered 'what if' she had been a guy or I a gurl.

2) Way back when, twins were seen as evil portents in parts of Nigeria. When they were born they were destroyed instantly, sometimes with their mother. Things have changed, twins are celebrated now, there is even a twin worshiping cult that sees us as 'spiritually powerful', 'tricksters', 'gifts from God', 'two halves of the same soul'.

3) I believe Nigeria's identity to be twinned; split between its indigenous population and its far reaching diasporic communities.

4) It is believed in parts of West Africa that children grow to embody their names, that a child named 'Joy' will spread happiness. This idea touched even Shakespeare. Cordelia (name means heart) was honest, loveable and the kindest sister in King Lear. Prospero prospered on the land he claimed, and Othello murdered Desdemona. 'Desdemona', derived from Greek, means 'ill fated'.

5) Keats also believed similarly saying 'Poets are midwives of reality'. Those who work with words call things into being.

6) In Hip Hop, the culture of taking on powerful pseudonyms is common. The public is forced to address rappers on their own grounds, complimenting and elevating them at once, imagine greeting: Good morning Mr Most Definitely / g'morning Mr Fabulous / Mr Immortal Technique / Mr Fantastic / Mr Black Thought.

7) Backtrack to birth, if Nigeria's reigns were given to its youth, entirely without an imposed destination, direction or expectation. If on their birthday, they were then asked to decide on their own path, to sculpt their own future. If a child was asked to 'name' itself, what would happen?..

*Inua Ellams, 2010*

*Untitled* was first performed at Bristol Old Vic on 23 September 2010.

*Written and performed by* Inua Ellams
*Directed by* Thierry Lawson
*Designed by* Peter Arnold
*Lighting Design by* Michael Nabarro
*Sound Design by* Emmanuel Lorien Spinelli
*Touring Production Manager* Ben Sherratt

# Act 1

## PART 1

*Stormy weather. A forest floor littered with a bag, a shirt, white stones, books, a bottle. The sound of struggle. X is chased onto the stage, dressed in old rolled up trousers, skin marked with abstract shapes, circles, dots. X shouts after a group of men...*

> / You foolish, backward, senile, old... no one can make any demands of me! Are you hearing? Not even the Spirits! Let this night pass and I'll be back with such strength, you'll regret this treatment of me! / Senile, small minded, bush men.../
>
> Eh?! There is always an audience. Always, Always, Always...

*X looks to the ground, notices his scattered belongings, gathers them into the bag, murmuring 'always, an audience...' he straightens up.*

> Always an audience eh? They say the walls have ears. Here, we also know that you the Spirits are listening! You correspond through leaves and bushes, curl them like ears, trap wind and whispering as willows or gossiping marigolds, swap our stories like seeds. We know. So, you must have heard of me now, what do you know? Oh, you don't have to say anything, Osalu taught me well, I can read...

*X looks about the stage, selects four leaves, reading each like braille. Between each leaf, he comments, setting them about the stage.*

Eh! Wait O! They were not naked! They only threw their waist beads! That is not true! / Ha! Again, you are mistaken, the soil is too rich! Get your facts right, Osalu asked me! / What! That just happened! Chai! News travels fast sha! Okay, okay / Eh, bloody ants making holes, it is like chewing through a letter! Disrespectful! / Okay, four stories to leaf through? four to clarify eh? Let us begin.

We have a tradition as old as the hills, started by the gods who drank oceans, pissed rivers and spat streams. Their practises would leak into dreams of men when they drank from them and that is how we know this was done... Now, when a child is born, the father and mother never speak the name of the son or daughter, chose only on paper and... wait, I am forgetting something... e he! We also believe that the sounds of words have power. To name something is to call it into life and determine its future, for instance, a child named 'Freedom' is destined to roam the world, so tremendous care is taken when naming. Now, when a child is born, the father and mother never speak the name of the son or daughter, choose only on paper. When it is settled and a name takes form, the child is carried into a clearing in the forest on the night of the first full moon, lifted to light and whispered its name, that it may first know its destiny and claim it before the world does.

I was born on Independence day, 1st of October. As Nigeria danced and villages pulsed with talking drums, I kicked into the world, but there were two of us. Identical twins. When my father who laboured far heard the news, he ran like a wind to the hut back home, for

the moon was two days away and he had to name two
sons. At night, he carried us gently, his bare feet crushed
the forest's green, my mother – one step behind him,
the path unwinding like a lock of hair to the clearing
where the moon swooned down and licked the lounging
leaves, passed me to my mother, lifted my brother
and whispered his name. He smiled, giggled a laugh
that tickled the moon who grew brighter for my turn,
father lifted me to light, made to say my name, when a
shadow crossed the moon for a fragment of an instance
and fled. The forest's heart skipped a beat that spread
into the undergrowth, rippled all trees. Father shivered,
waited for the moment to pass, then lifted me to light,
whispering my name…

WHAAAAAAAAAAAAAAAA! I cried! I screamed!
So loudly, the stream ran back to the river, the moon
dimmed, the bushes curled back their ears, animals
fled the forest, the village thought The End had come.
WHAAAAAAAAAAA! That night I woke up the world!
It had never passed in the village that a child rejected its
destiny, its name. Father tried six more times to name
me, each time I screamed till the Spirits cringed, seven
months, seven moons in total. After that, he gave up
// Let him name himself for all I care! // Mother was
unhappy // The Spirits will not stand for it, there will
be consequences // she warned… they argued, they
fought. Bitterly. He struck her. She carried my brother
and left the village. The elders said that as our parents
pulled us apart, we cried my brother and I. Our screams
splintered young trees, split two kola nuts and froze the
blood as they watched. We were just seven months old.

The elders were so ashamed they kept it a secret. That was twenty five years ago, haven't seen them since. So, I grew up a child with no destiny, the unnamed one. That is how life began.

*Sound of a party, a celebration in the distance.*

Ah?! The celebrations, okay quick, next story, next story, em... Okay, this one.

## PART 2

*X chooses another set, puts the leaf in his bag, holds the stone to the light, begins...*

Because of my namelessness, father was deemed a failure in the eyes of the men and after mother vanished he'd leave me on my own. I'd scavenge around for food running wild through the village. Some women would pity and care for me, but when their children laughed that I hadn't a single name, I'd lash out hard and they'd throw me out again.

The last who tried to care for me was married to a storyteller and I used to train with him. One night, he taught me the story of the tortoise's cracked back. One day tortoise lied that his name was 'Everybody'. The cook came out announcing 'There is food for everybody' and Tortoise ate everything! So angered by his greed, they threw him off a tree. His shell smashed and till this day tortoise has a cracked back. The moral is okay, you know, but the tortoise showed that I could takes names as I wished.

10 years old, I'd turned a hard-soled ruffian slouched in the shade of the mango tree at the market place. It is a tumultuous nightmare, oceans of clashing fabrics storm the eye. Goat herds coast past the myriad of people, the dust kicked up by hurrying feet form a cloud of fine gold through which the sellers beat – both young and old, tins to the rhythm of their wares... Groundnuts! Fresh Fish! Fried Locusts! Fried Locusts! The heat is thick, the grass-roof shacks are singed with it, Mrs Ogholi the dried pepper seller is there with her bad breath fuming out of her. Mrs Okpah the corn seller is dodging her bad breath like bullets, Mrs Amayo arranges her cocoyams into neat and perfect piles, and Miss Abaogo whose smile wets the dreams of men, warms her cassava by the fire, and I'm there, waiting, watching everything. Mrs Ogholi sends her servant, I intercept with...

aayss ssss, small boy, ehe, what is this? / Dried pepper for Mr Okpalie? / yes, I am Mr Okpalu's son. / Ah yes now, that is my name ah ah?... / what do you mean prove it? / okay what is my name then? you don't know... aha, see now, / oya, drop it, go, go, we will send the money later... / – (*Aside.*) foolish boy.

ehe, you, better boy / wetin be that? / cocoyams for Mr Mankwa? / ah he told me to thank her / Yes, I am his son Emmanuel Mankwa yes oh / Okay drop it, move on... / eh you...

Within three hours I could have opened my own shop: A pouch of snuff, a bunch of bitter leaf, fresh palm oil, plenty palm wine, fish caked in salt so it won't spoil, the

peppers, the cassava, the corn. But I failed to factor in
Mr Mankwa who sprouted out of nowhere...

Mrs Amayo, where are my cocoyams? / to my son / ah?
I don't have a son / by which mango tree? / ah! look
how much goods he has! he could open his own shop...

and in no time at all a widening arch of sellers
surrounded, scowling, pointing, shouting, fingers
stabbing the air. The charge was ridiculous, I was
found guilty of 'corrupting our traditional folk stories
and using it solely for the advancement of ones
own personal gain and interests'. Father grew even
more distant and left me to the discipline of elders. I
remember, the moon rose strict and dominant like a
judge presiding over the village, the wind – its jury,
whistled with the stale sweat of the elders in the hut
where it poked me, angry in a corner; the stolen wares
scattered around. The hut smelt of wood and fire. Elder
Mgoda, the legendary hunter, with his long sleek nose,
spoke first.

// Eh... we know the story of this boy but we cannot
tell his destiny, he remains unnamed till this day. We
declined from telling the villagers and look what he has
done! Now we must tell them! // – Elder Samsa agreed
– // Yes, and punish him too! We must...// Ah... said
Mgoda, we mustn't anger him // What? he is only a boy
now ah a he is only a boy, // Yes, but we cannot tell his
destiny, look into his eyes, even before me, Mgoda, he
is fearless! We know not his future, we must be careful,
eh Osalu, what do you think? //

And Osalu whose eyes had never left the palm wine, looked to the elders and blinked. Osalu was ours, the most famous medicine man, famed throughout the land if not for his powerful skills, then for his love of palm wine. Such was his fondness that most times, he'd drink to excess at night and charge around the village wrestlers singing – *start the fight, start the fight, start the fight…*

// Eh? / – Osalu said – / Yes, his future is clouded. Until we know more, let us exercise caution. He is clearly wise beyond his years, will probably corrupt our stories so, let him exercise biceps instead of his brains. Let him learn the trade of the drum. //

At first the drummers were reluctant, but I didn't care – those bare chested baboons couldn't tell a fork from a spoon – but Osalu explained the problem of my name and all except one, agreed. Soon I'd swooned into the squadron of boys with thick shoulders and low songs, who'd see the crack of dawn before the cock crowed and sun glowed, would journey into the forest and by the dim glow of logs, tell masculine stories of violence. The crack of fire would spark the air and meet the moonlight's steady glare, where Bolu the leader, would beat his chest and say // Drummers! // – We'd reply, // Yah! // The way of the drum is the way of life if you disagree move out of here! //

There were seven of us. Bolu, Obina, Badboy, Esu, Samson, Kika and me. I taught them the slouch of the mango tree and the camaraderie that spun between us seemed tighter than fingers form fists. Apart from Kika

– a little too pristine, we formed a rabble of boys who'd lift logs, beat songs, hunt for the finest skins, this too is the way of the drum.

// Drummers // – We'd reply, // Yah! // A drummer must always keep time, and know the strike of his fists for a perfect blow can disrupt the flow of a warrior's hearts beat / now in the heat of a drum pattern, the Spirits of the drum can come. When they call your name allow them in, let them control your form. //

But, I am the nameless one. Ha!

As the years passed and our grasp of the drum deepened into its subtle forms, we began slipping into Spirits. I remember Samson's back stiffened, his eyes grew dark as storms, his shoulders froze rigid, but his arms loosened like worms and seemed to wind through the spine of the drum, ba da bo bo de ba de bi dum, then Badboy mastered the spine of the drum, then Esu, Obina even Kika. But when the sprits came my way, they were baffled I hadn't a name and in their confusion, I stole their rhythms for my own personal gain – when they played a deep mountain song, I'd sprinkle out a stream, when the Spirits beat out earth and fire, I'd drum the substance of dreams! Ha! This created a dynamic that only lived in us and news spread through villages that new music had come. Our sound moved the spirits of the people and their bodies barely held on, they danced and twirled as if their veins pumped storms and when I began to play with my counter spiritual rhythms, Hey! It wrenched their souls apart and the women turned primal, such hunger in their eyes. Kika disliked this...

// Listen, boys, before this goes too far, we must keep within the rhythm, the Ancient Spirits are... // BORING! // – I said casting his words aside – // the Spirits are boring, we make the people happy, they dance with joy, what can be wrong? Eh...? Ah... Kika just shut up, I have mastered their rhythms, those Spirits are just dead old men, they can't touch me! // – Kika tried a different approach, but the boys were inclined with me. He spoke not one more word, turned and walked away.

Those were the days! We travelled the plains playing at harvests, new moon and new rain festivals, for chiefs, champions and children. I saw my father a few times, but he'd just shake his head and turn. But I didn't care, we had groups of girls who'd scream when they'd see us and throw their waist beads, one almost blinded Obina, foolish girl! Everyone knew our names – apart from me, but a small price to pay because I was the most remembered, the famous nameless one! Kika became assistant leader and he took to shouting out orders, barking the other's names. His dislike of my rhythms turned a jealous hatred, and I angered him further. When he tried to get my attention, he'd begin // you there / boy / erm / chai / whoooe / ssssss / *(Snapping fingers.)* / drummer, drummer! // – I'd wait till he'd exhaust all attempts, calmly turn and say – // Eh?! //

It was the month of harvest, we were to play at the feast, there was a prize for the finest drum, I was determined to win. The prize? A date with the chief's daughter, Ovelaenu – the beautiful, whose name means 'the bright moon', who Kika liked too. The village was a flurry of activities, pots of egusi soup bubbled as the laughter of children chasing chickens mixed with the soft thud of pounded yams vibrating up the trees bringing this background music to us – the boys gathered around, Bolu inspecting our handiwork, his face clear and proud:

// Samson, I like the subtle stain with soot fading from black to brown / Esu, you've crowned the drums with feathers, it shouldn't harm the sound / Obi, your use of cowrie shells has made me come around / Badboy, that's good / Kika your detailed use of chalk; precise patterns I've never seen before / and eh you, no, not you, you, YOU ehe… what is that? // Ah Bolu! I'm only half done, this drum makes the finest sound, as for presentation, I am coming back! //

I left the baffled drummers and ran the thick forest grabbing wild flowers, potent herbs, weeds, petals and stems, rich leaves and scented roots till I could hold no more, tore back to the clearing planning to lace the shell of the drum, so each strike would free the fumes, fill the judge's lungs with the thick musk of forest, a good plan… no? As I scattered past the drummers dropping leaves this way and that, a few landed by Kika who particularly pernickety that day screamed…

//aesssss / ssss / PICK IT UP // a ah? Kika… just kick it now // NO! COME AND PICK IT UP. // Kika I don't have time for this I have to // COME BACK

HERE pick it up! Who do you think you are? // I
am the nameless one // 'I am the nameless one' SO
WHAT?! think you are special? I voted against you
joining us, Yes it was me! And now you have a big head,
you brotherless bastard! // WHAT did you call me! //
Ah? did I stutter? we all know your story, your mother
grabbed your brother and left, you father doesn't care.
You are alone in the world, I am just calling you what
you are – you brotherless bast… //

I struck him to the ground! He rose up like a panther
and the battle began. Esu shredded away the feathers
and began a fearsome drum pattern making our blood
boil. The boys clamoured around as Bolu tried to keep
the peace, but they'd tired of Kika's dominance so
this, was it. Kika dove right, I feigned left, tripped him
as he stumbled past, he threw sand in my eyes and
pounced screaming "Brotherless bastard!" And I struck
with blind madness as if I fought the world, struck till
he fell and even then I carried on… It ended with the
boys staring to the ground as I struck Kika into stillness
before Bolu dragged me down. I couldn't explain my
anger, power, rage. I wasn't pleased with what I'd done,
but it was known from that day on, the strength of the
nameless one!

*There is a sudden, deafening crack of thunder and lightning…*

Ah a storm? At this time of year? The celebrations! The
hunters are coming! I don't have time O! Okay, Okay,
next story? Which one?

## PART 3

*X grabs another set, leaf in his bag, stone to light, and begins…*

Ehe! I did not beg, Osalu asked me!.. Okay, I'll start at the beginning / There's an old proverb: the lizard that jumps from the tallest tree applauds himself if no one else will. I applauded myself after Kika. No one else did.

// He is no longer welcome. // Bolu said so in the shade of the Silk-Cotton tree where Spirits of unborn children are said to live. It was night and the moon was a cutlass slashing through branches cutting his words to sharp shards that pierced me.

// He is no longer welcome, what he did to Kika, it is never done. // Kika, whose face had swelled like a bullfrog coughed from the corner // Daily he defies the Spirits and defies me! Who does he… // Kika shut up // said Bolu // Shut up! Elders, he is not welcome in the circle of drums, I have never seen such violence, such… until we know more of his destiny, he is dangerous. That is all. //

The drummers left the shade. The seven elders sank into their chairs, my smashed drum before them, its strong forest flower scents slowly dying out. In the silence I heard the silk tree whispering, but when I turned it stopped. Osalu looked up.

// Leave him with me // What? // asked Mgoda // Why? What can you do that we haven't done? // My ways are not your ways Mgoda, I am Osalu! I have forgotten more than you know. I have asked, if need be, I shall demand, leave him with me. // Okay, Samsa, Kwendo, Ide, Igbekhai, Ogbaki... let us go //

The elders lifted their goatskin bags, drinking horns and left. The night was clear. The crickets chorused, other insects filled the air, the moonlight caressed each living thing, the Silk-Cotton tree glistening like rain had fallen there. A low wind whistled with this forest's music and Osalu breathed in...

// I knew your mother / Yes, yes, a good woman... / You have refused a name since birth, refused everything tried on you, only the men of your blood line can name you and your father washed his hands. The reason you fought Kika lies in his words... they come close to defining you – a brother without a brother and parents who parted ways, I understand your actions... Still it was wrong. / So... why did you pick these plants? / Yes the one around the drum here / Answer my question. / I am Osalu, I do not explain myself to... / I AM OSALU, I HAVE FORgotten more... / I am an old man, answer my questions, please / You mean you did not plan it? / The herbs to ease his injuries? / The black leaf there stopped his face swelling. If Bolu hadn't applied it, he would have... / The juice of that green root revived him from stillness... you mean it was by chance / Ha! Wonders shall never end! / Okay... no one will, so I must do it. I, Osalu will train you, you will be the next medicine man. //

Gossip spread like wild fire, 'Osalu is training the nameless one, the man who knows all destinies trains the boy without none!' Ha! The villagers talked of

nothing else, took bets that he'd fail, but he laughed
their talk away saying // We shall see, We shall see //

Years passed, Osalu taught me many things. He said
// Humanity is the point in time when nature realised
it exists. The world is one living thing, at all times
listening, if you learn the forest's way, you can fix the
world! You know *Agbighouzo,* that white-sap thick leaf?..
You know it now? Aha! ehe, lightly roast before rubbing
onto broken bones, it speeds up healing a hundred fold
– the wide stemmed *Obieru,* chew with alligator pepper,
spit onto chests and it eases fevers, and its root – soaked
in hot water or mixed with palm wine... that unwinds
aches and pains like that! //

But these only deal with physical things. Osalu talked of
the Spirits. He said // if you look at a stone and cover it,
the image still lives in the mind's eye. That is the Spirit
of stone. And everything, caves, harvests, new moons,
everything has a spirit. And always the spirit-world sits
on our own. Now, in the halfway times, in the doorways
of huts, waist deep in water, when sun shines and
rain falls, in these half times, the line between worlds
are thin and Spirits can pass into the minds of men,
become trapped in them, angry, violent and it is the job
of medicine men to lead Spirits back to their land. //
Osalu was famed for this, his soothing-spirits-skills were
legendary... But I had a different skill, to play the spirit
of a drum!

Guided by Osalu, I honed my ways and we began
to work together. Instantly fame came. The villagers
apologised for doubting Osalu, who just smiled into

his horn of palm wine and raised the price! We were so sought after, we had to work apart. My patients would wake from their spirit-stupor talking of drums, wake with such clarity, they'd mix my rhythm with their stories. This re mix would go from tongue to tongue with tales of the nameless one; I became more famous than Osalu! It's true what they say – the young rises when the old falls eh? I had so many jobs I'd cast aside the cheap ones for lesser medicine men, only accepted the rich people who addressed me well. They must come with four chickens, three goats, two kola nuts, one horn of wine and ask / Excuse me Sir, are you the famous nameless one? / to which I say / I am / Anyone who got it wrong, I wouldn't treat, ignore or even curse. And why not?

Travelling palm wine sellers were a cause for gatherings as they carried stories and songs wherever they went, back to my village to the elders, where Osalu, mostly out of work was angered by my fame. His tongue, loosened by wine condemned every song, telling the seller to // Shut up! I am Osalu, I trained him. You know not what you speak, he is still a novice, hardly knows the Spirit world. That brotherless bastard would still be… Ehe? I called him a brotherless bastard… oh, you don't know his story? Ah! Well he was born to a… What is it Mgoda?… We shouldn't tell strangers about… sit down Mgoda, it is common knowledge here, might as well be everywhere. Now he was born to a… // Osalu told him everything.

None of this I knew as I passed through a village, a foolish idiot boy approached me with just two

chickens and a mango! // Excuse, you are him? ehe,
can you treat my mother? she is possessed by a snake
spirit and // GET OUT OF MY WAY, IF YOU DO
NOT KNOW THE PROPER RITES THEN FIND
SOMEONE ELSE / What do I care if you haven't
eaten for days? / Listen, I don't have time for you,
commot for road, NOW! before I // Okay, I'm going,
Brotherless Bastard… think you are // WHAT DID
YOU SAY // he ran as I gave chase through the village
shouting // Help! The brotherless bastard is after me //
The entire village spilled out chanting 'Bastard go away!
I tumbled from the weight of names onto the forest
floor.

The trees whispered amongst themselves as a fever
gripped me. That night I shivered by firelight. The
cold moon rose and watched wondering what I'd do
as I chewed and spat leaf after leaf seeking the right
medicine. The day, dawned in the forest, found a dead
fire and a medicine man marching vengefully home.
Osalu and the village would pay.

*X picks up the last stone. Crunches up the leaf.*

I returned and waited for the moon, climbed the
hollow of the Silk-Cotton tree and each night played
the drum, played the rhythm that wrenched souls apart
and turned the women primal. Such want would grip
them, the men could never satisfy. Months I played far
into the night till a barren year passed and no woman
had a child. Around me, the Silk tree shrivelled and
dried as Spirits of unborn children died. The eve of
independence, of my birthday came when the whole

country danced, but still I played, hotter, faster till
at dusk, Ovelaenu burst from her hut, fuelled by the
pattern of the soul-wrenched drum chased by Kika her
husband and other villagers. That is how they found
me, late last night curled in the womb of the dead
cotton tree.

They dragged me to Osalu who shook with anger
// YOU HAVE DONE IT NOW! The Spirits have
cursed you: you have been given one week, seven days
in which to be named, otherwise you and your entire
blood line shall be wiped off the face of the earth! Till
then, you are banished! GET HIM OUT OF HERE //

And those foolish, backward, senile, old… / no one can
make any demands of me! Are you hearing? Not even
the Spirits! Let this night pass and I'll be back with such
strength, you'll regret this treatment of me! / A name,
you senile, small minded, bush… / Spirits do your
worst!

*X roams about the stage seething, muttering to himself as storm clouds gather. There is a burst of lightning in which he is struck down. He falls. BLACK OUT.*

*END OF FIRST ACT*

# ACT2

*X gets up slowly and puts on a shirt and tie, walks around the circle, in so doing he becomes the twin brother in London, Y, he walks about the stage talking as if reading from a dairy.*

### Day 1. Friday.

The city of London, like a concrete forest sprawls in
dizzying dips and dives that rise like mountains, at times
like hills, all else is battle ground. Rippling reels of
cheap film tell a tangled tale of bustling lifestyles, streets
chaos-thick with commerce busting from window sills.
Snapshot: A coffee cup. A beggar's crusted knuckles.
A wallet fat with bills. An even fatter corporate cat, a
sex kitten at his heels. A cyclist breaks from this craze,
leaves the neon lights, its glaring haze for the residential
chaos of tower blocks stuffed, some with crying
children, some with cooling fists and trembling women,
a stones throw from rich homes where the abuse is
different.

The moon, fails to spread its calm to this city. It waits,
as mosquito-like, an airplane tinkles by, takes a deep
breath then sends its moonshine diving for the city with
the swifts, swallows and sways with mists and pirate
radio waves, enters an office block by its window pane,
slides across a carpet, hushes up a table, smoothes the

sleeping skin of the dozing fellow. Lithe and finger-light, the moon rests on my neck.

Lightning shoots out of me into the silver keyboard, strides down its wires, fries the hard drive, all burns electric blue bristling with fire. Milly on the desk beside snaps back and screams, spilling coffee across her Filofax.

Maxwell, my boss, comes swinging from his office with others like followers funnelling behind down the centre isle of the open plan space. They gather round my desk, check that I'm all right. And I know some are disappointed that I am. Apart from Virginia, my laptop who died, whose soul is the solder-smoke drifting up the aisle, I tell them // I'm okay… perfectly fine. //

Max, who knows I love my work, thinks I tell a lie, straightens up his tie, sends me home. // It's your birthday // he says. I look up surprised // Go home, relax, besides, it's overtime. // I wipe down my table, set-right the phone so it sits parallel with the Post It Notes and stacks of lined paper by the paper weight stones, take up my bag and leave.

I go to a night club, and find its dance-floors heaving, filled with pulsing Nigerians celebrating the 1st of October, Independence, my birthday. The Dj spins 50 cent's classic hit, the dancers replace 'Shorty' with 'Naija' so the rough chorus is remixed to this: "Go Nija, it's your birthday, we gon' party like its your birthday, gon' sip Bacardi like it's your birthday, and you know we don't give a fuck it's not your…" caught in the sway of bodies, I imagine 'Nija' is swapped for my name and the gathered dancers celebrate me... but when the chorus comes, my head starts to swim just as it did at the office. I leave.

Outside, the streets are lined with trees and the trees, they rustle as if in sympathy; leaves stroking paving stones. They walk me to the station. Home, I brush my teeth, check my temperature is fine, pupils react to light, have their normal shine, climb into bed, ready myself to sleep. And I can't help but feel, as if a conscience were shifted a little to the left or a speck of dust pricked a white sheet, can't help but feel that something is wrong.

### Day 2. Saturday.

I wake to ten missed calls from mum, call back, no answer. I begin my day, clean the flat, do laundry. Take clothes out of my wardrobe, fold neatly back in. Thirty press-ups, twenty sit-ups, ten sets to keep trim. Kitchen. Three eggs. Great source of protein. Think if you break the word, you get 'pro' and 'tein', it helps to build muscle strength, keeps one young. Protein is Pro Teen. I scribble this on Post Its, add to others on the fridge which rustles; a bush of broken words and meanings, each Post It flutters, crisp as a leaf.

Evening, I go jogging, run through side streets and alleys, duck under archways, vault flights of stairs, I cough out the smoggiest of London's atmosphere, arrive at the park and start to time laps. I fly past mothers, rollerbladers and strollers, lovers trying to catch what summer is left. Lap two, a dog owner bends to scoop her prize. Lap three, a pedestrian steps in dog-surprise.

Lap four, it starts as a slow hum. Lap five, it sharpens to a knife of noise. Lap six, its a stream now a constant whispering. Lap seven, it's a river swell, a hissing wall, swords of sighing voices snarling from the green. I jog through the gate, past the park's railings and it stops. Not a murmur, not a sound.

### Day 3. Sunday.

After a good night's dream in which I romanced the moon, I convince myself: yesterday was nothing. I go to the library to return books and renew the first edition of 'Tractatus', Wittgenstein's work on the links between language and reality, words and how they mean. I leave the library and though I'm sure it's fine, avoid the park and walk the stone streets. At night before I sleep, I'm drawn to the window, where a man nails a flier to a tree. With each hammer's strike, I hear, though it's muffled, a clear audible and terrified scream.

### Day 4. Monday.

London grumbles to life through oncoming autumn and fading lights. Bikers knife through clogged traffic with cyclist pedal-quick, clicking at their heels. At work, a project to brand a chain of florists finds each table laden with bouquets and vases, releasing their scents up and out. The air-con systems cools and carries so a nectar scented petal thick breeze leads me down the wide centre aisle.

On the right there's Cynthia, short skirt, red lips, talking to Kofi, stroking his knees. Left, there's Adam

six ft three, babbling in Japanese to overseas clients.
Behind him, Ally who is overqualified, but loves to
research passionately as I. Right, Dana, startling grey
eyes, there's Farzad, Katie, Lizzibeth, Tim and ten or
so others filtering in and beside my table but across
the aisle, there's Milly. She looks up, smiles. I sit
and wonder where music is coming from. Only then
discover that as I walked down the aisle, the sound –
like chamber choirs – came from the flowers. I reach to
ask Milly if she hears it, then stop. What if she doesn't?
Remember the park?

By the day's end, I feel sick. Balls of crushed tissue
fountain from my ears. The chamber music is now a
funeral song and a vengeful ache pounds against my
skull. I grit my teeth through the last thirty minutes,
sweat dripping in the freezing office. I pick up my bag
and make for the lift. As I pass the flower song scrapes
up to me, I try to walk but my vision tunnels to a point
and the wide centre aisle stretches to a mile, I break into
a jog, swearing with pain, but stagger to the ground and
crawl to the lift. The whole office stands to their feet,
pointing, Milly rushes forward, I tell her to // Stay Back
// Max comes out as the lift door closes. I reach the
ground floor, hit the stone streets, station, home, pills,
sleep.

### Day 5. Tuesday.

I wake with a fever and arrive at work late. The flowers
are gone, but everything aches and water funnels down
my face. It's morning break so the room is half empty
and thankfully beside me, Milly isn't here. By lunch

time my dustbin overflows Kleenex, clumps of damp tissue, my table reeks of sweat. It drips from my fingers soaks anything I write so each pen stroke rips the sheets of research. I give up and wear a pair of gloves instead. When Max nods in my direction, unthinkingly, I wave, till he frowns. I put my hand abruptly down. He comes to my desk, rests on the table, checks if tomorrow's meeting is as scheduled. 9.00 am, his office. I nod to confirm, wipe my face and look down until he turns.

I get home at seven and my fever's worsened to boiling hot flushes and violent shakes. Between wet flannels and ice cold showers, I try to call mum for a traditional remedy; her clay cups of herbs, stems and leaves. But her phone rings and rings. She's always at home I think. Too uncomfortable, too flustered, to sleep, I try all night companioned by the moon who watches, a worried search light my twistings on the sheets. At 6 a.m. the phone is answered, a gruff male voice says // Come quick. //

## PART 2

### *Day 6. Wednesday.*

I arrive at mum's flat first thing, walk past the failing flora outside, the scattered scraggy grass struggles to live like malnourished children with half formed limbs. The tower block reeks of weeks of stale urine, clumps of used condoms, needles and spliffs. Fourth floor, I remember her bell doesn't work, reach to knock, but the door swings open wide and a wall of boiling air near knocks me off my feet. I stagger into the room surprised that I leave footprints and notice the floor is covered in soil. The lights are off, but the naked light bulb above fountain sparks onto a figure on the floor, buried neck to feet with a quilt of wet leaves, steam rising off the dark cover with a low hum ringing round my knees. // Can you hear them my son? can you hear them sing? // And I am silenced, too stunned to speak.

When speech returns, I lunge for her, ripping off leaves. A man from a corner tackles me to the floor. We struggle, I'm trying to get to mum and we crash against the table, knock black candles to the floor, lumps of white chalk, crushed nuts, palm oil, stuff soaked in bowls of cold water, some sort of incense thick to the nose, we battle scattering left right and rip clumps of dark feathers tied to white sticks. A woman from the kitchen appears and screams // STOP! eh! Look! // I turn, mum quivers out to me. I rush forward // My son... I don't have much time... Listen... your brother...has... you have to... Osalu said... // Mum, what's wrong? DON'T TOUCH HER!! Sshh, don't speak, I'll call an ambul... // NO! listen, remember, you have to reach the village... the story is real. Do as Osalu says... It is your destiny. My son don't question me, his ways are not our ways, just go... please... you have to name him, the story is REAL! // Her cough grows to a violent fit, the wet leaves shifting reptilian in the dark. Without warning her arm goes limp. // Mum... is she? //

The man I fought against lifts me to my feet. // We will do our best. Now, take this. // He thrusts an envelope into my chest, pushes me protesting out the front door.

Outside, I bang till my fists go numb, rip the envelope, find a plane ticket to Nigeria, dated to leave tonight and something scrawled in mother's hand, 'Remember the story'. That's all.

I lean and vomit from the fourth floor, blood rushes, pounds my ear drums. When it fades, it is replaced by everything screaming, I can hear them clear. Oak trees in the distance, the dying autumn leaves, strangled plant-pots like stolen children, the traffic islands, the allotments plotting, green houses and gardens, roots and weeds, all the suffocating tortured flora of London, wailing, baying out to me. I wrap arms around my head and leave, stagger down the high street, crash through pedestrians, making for the station.

Underground, I am coffined by stone and steel, here, there's silence enough to think. Last time she told the story I was seventeen; of a ceremony scattered in a forest, and a twin brother with no destiny. The train comes and pulls out of the station, the clattering rail mere humdrum to me till I exit at work and the trees begin to screech.

I walk out the lift, down the wide isle to my desk where, Max, smiles // You're always on time. // This way he says gesturing to his office. I sit in the room, but I'm miles away, words churning ...brother...destiny... name. // Now, how is the current project going? The florists? do you have something for us? // I snap back to Max, focusing on the room, at dictionaries and phrase books, stacks of market graphs, the cork board riddled with lists of the worst gaffes in car branding history:

How General Motors produced the Chevy Nova, but in Spanish 'Nova' means 'Won't do' or The Ford 'Pinto', hatchback car – but 'pinto' is slang for small genitalia // Max raps his knuckles on the table. // Florist? Do you have a name? // Destiny... all my life I've trained... // Max interrupts.. // Are you okay? Do you know where you? // Peacocks, we are a strategic agency. We advise brands on how to sell things. We research markets and culture trends, we develop products, their look and feel, all before it's Prototype-ed and Pdf-ed to me! Max, I specialise in the naming of things... / Max, sorry, I need to go. / No / I mean now / To Nigeria / No! Not next week / No, you are not listening, it's a NEED / No, NOW, it's... family! THE FLORISTS CAN WAIT! // Max stands slowly, holding a pair of scissors, turns his back to me, to his banzai tree, its pride of place a stand by the window sill and begins. Instantly my head starts to swim // Do you know you are lucky to have this job? // As he clips, the banzai tree screams // Max stop. // Graduates will kill for your job, You are good, brilliant, but quite replaceable... // Max stop! You are hurting it! // But Max in ranting ignores me, blades slicing at the tree's limbs // I dart forward to grab the pair of scissors. He struggles, we tussle, lose balance and fall. When I stand, there is blood on my hand, the scissors slashed through Max's white shirt.

I hold my head, wiping his blood on my face, trembling in the quiet of his office. He moves! He moans, sitting up off the floor. // Max? // He pulls back and shouts // GET OUT // I breeze out the door, down stairs to the streets, past the wailing trees and hail a black cab. Down

the M4, I rock back and forth thinking // Destiny...
brother... blood... name... // a furious fever erupts, I
convulse in the back seat, on both sides the M4 roars
and shrieks: a million blades of grass howling at me,
head bursts, too loud too hard to breath, throat tightens,
face strains, I gag... faint.

I wake to the cabbie tapping the window pane // We
are here // The airport holds back the pain, glass and
concrete shield me again. We fly at night, the moonlight
strokes my cheek, I think of mum as London shrinks
beneath, darkness swallows it as I fall to sleep.

### Day 7. Thursday.

The Lagos heat whips me incessantly, as if it alone
knows my guilt. I stand a stranger in my mother's land,
feeling the voice of its flora beneath. The custom officer
snarls in pidgin English // Oga, settle me // I give him
every penny and he fast tracks me past the winding visa
queues, crates of contraband, foul mouthed traders,
chiefs, tourists, students, thieves and deportees, past
the plaited mayhem of the busy airport, to the gates.
Here a crooked car waits, a bare footed man steps out
and sneers // You look just like him. Oya enter let's go.
// As we leave, I feel the flora's groans take hold and
I'm swallowed into a never where of dark stars and
earthenware, dust and bones crumble like skeletons
of words, half matter, half thought, they come for
me stronger in the wide open rows between huts and
houses on the dust tarred-roads, I slip out of focus, skin
sizzling heat. Hours pass, the car gasps up a forest's
hill. I tremble, delirious in the back seat. The driver

turns manic, a glint cuts his eye // Drink this / he says / you'll be alright // I gulp down the contents of the clay cup, but the flora's thoughts heighten tumultuous, hot, twisted like fear set free and I drown, buried in the back seat.

When I come to, a storm rumbles in the distance, lightning licks the clouds like a viper does its fangs. I'm flat on the ground, six drummers surround, strike a cruel beat with palms and finger tips, each strike quakes the ground, snakes up my arm till my heart beats in time to its question, an old man dances with the wild about him, spits chewed leaves, jumping over me. I try to stand // YOU'RE NOT READY! Elders hold him down // and six men restrain my chest, legs and arms // The forest calls out to me; chest burns, head churns, I want for the trees, for the leaf-rooted undergrowth, the dark bark, the decaying carpet of fungus, weeds, what poisons may flower, what fruits may feed! The old man stops, points to the sky and a shadow falls across the moon's face. I hear leaves flap like broken wings beating, flying out to me, I fight against the men, tear off my shirt, gasp as chalk marks burst from my skin, break from their grip and sprint. The moon hears me scream: a wild thing wounded flutters for the forest. I blast past farmlands, stone circles, I weave, an image comes of a Silk-Cotton tree, a mound of leaves and he is buried beneath.

I fall on top of it, gasping, chest heaves, the soil fills my mouth, my breath is of the earth, my tongue is of the fallen, the might-bes and forgotten, the roots wrap thick around my wrists, thorns pierce with sap, my

veins pump with it. The storm comes, a wind shredding
through trees, and I churn destiny…. brother….
name…. DESTINY… BROTHER…. NAME….
ARGGHHHHHHHhhh!

*The storm rages… Y is passed out on the ground. Fade to black.*

# Act 3

*Day 8. Friday.*

*Lights fade up slowly and X stands up as snatched phrases float through the air:*

> The spirits will not stand for this (Mother) // We know
> not his future, we must be careful (Mgoda) // My ways
> are not your ways (Osalu) // The Spirit of the Drums
> can come (Bolu) // Thunder // Do as Osalu says...
> (Mother) // YOU ARE NOT READY Elders Hold him
> down // You have to name him, the story is REAL!
> (Mother) // It is your destiny (Mother) // Are you
> ready?... (Y)

> The elders say he ran through the forest, wind howling
> through trees, lightning licking leaves as he flashed past;
> saw the husk of the silk cotton tree, the mound of leaves
> I was buried beneath and thrust his hands through the
> soil. They say it happened in the blink of an eye, but for
> us it lasted a life time.

> I was half dead. Yes. My spirit had started to seep into
> the stream but when he thrust through the soil, his
> hands found mine and what roots remained of the silk
> cotton tree tied our wrists together and his spirit became
> mine as I became his.

The sky blinked, and in the half dark, the line between worlds were thin. We merged with the moon spirit and understood many things. I lived his memories as he lived mine; saw his loneliness as a child, he wept as father left and I spent nights alone. I cried when I saw mother, her skin cold as stone. Had I known they were alive, I would not have risked...

// But there is time // he said. And as we shared stories, he'd weave together thoughts. As if making medicine, he tied the roots of words and buried beneath the soil, I saw the sounds take form. We let them slip across our lips and there they grew strong, we opened our mouths together and one word leapt off our tongues.

Then he pulled me from the ground, soil falling off my skin. The silk cotton tree burst back to life and the forest filled with whispering.

He wants to find our father, mother will be here in days. We want to tell the story of how we built a name.

*Black out.*

*THE END.*

KNIGHT WATCH

*Knight Watch* was first performed at Greenwich + Docklands international Festival on 23 June 2012.

*Written and performed by* Inua Ellams
*Directed by* Thierry Lawson
*Original Music by* Zashiki Warashi

"...from now on cities will be built on one side of the street so that soothsayers will have wilderness to wander and lovers space enough to contemplate a kiss..."

*Saul Williams, said the shotgun to the head*

All candles are cousins of the sun.
The moon plays foster mother. The waters swear
always to reflect her light. Dust is daughter to
these givers of life, all grandmother'd by nature
holding tight. In this patch-work order, this
unclear night, we all are prodigal sons; we alone
journey to spirit city, but earth remains our home
and scattered, we live across its round dome. We
live in wilderness where vultures coast the sky,
where sand storms, the land is worn, the river
beds dry and lush forests where rain torrents and
birds cloud the sky, where herds stampede past
trees, feed on bountiful evergreens…

But mostly we live in cities where we can't see
stars for fumes, so turn to smashed glass, believing
shards shine like constellations do. We disregard
the sun and the moon who lights us when the
dark looms, instead bow to cement and steel, to
stone pollen and refined minerals that combined,
make mountains that scrape the sky.

In the South East side of one such city lived two tribes, two constant rivals. First was the 'House of Herne' known for bank thievery and slow dealing, for crisp shirts, strict appearances and clipped speech. Slow to anger and slow to forgive, they rose to power in the late Nineties, followed close by the 'Knights of Newtown', the boisterous, brick-built, back street boys, known for loose clothes, deep throats and insults, quick to anger and quick to forgive, they worked in burglaries but ruled the drug deals.

This caused the quarrel. The House wanted the drug market for their own, but The Knights never wished to relinquish the throne. The battles over this were so subscribed to, that almost overnight, after scuffles, graffiti tapestries of fight scenes would be found sprayed on the sprawling urban walls.

I lived amongst The Knights in one tower block, one stone mountain circled by grey mists. I never joined the tribe, so became an outcast, they called me "the young fool" who lived in the past.

I lived alone and for stretches of days the only living things I'd see were trees. And in those days landscaped by stone and steel, those grey mornings and greyer nights, torch-lit by darker thrills, trees were dwindling single things; like me, last rebels from an age long gone, endangered in this city of dust and nylon. If I ever found one, I'd try to help it live. If it died, I'd take it home, wait till it dried and shape into any object I desired. So through me, dead trees would keep living. My first sculptures were small figurines, then palm-sized, then desk-sized and varied in between, but my greatest undertaking was a whole wooden car. It had wooden wheels, wooden tyres, wooden seats, wooden engine, wooden pistons, wooden doors, wooden forks but when I tried it, the car wouldn't work.

Searching for wood one autumn night, I chanced across a disturbance by one small tribe that shattered constellations of glass in bar fights. I was alone and must have seemed like easy prey; the tribe circled me silently, the breeze blew in sympathy. I knew I couldn't run, so though frightened stayed my ground as the nearest one threatened:

"gimme your money, if you don't wanna die"


with a knife in the street light, flashing before my
eyes, I told him all I had was bus fare home. But
this just angered him, his voice grew louder, his
hand shook, he demanded I shut up, advanced
with a dark look. I gave him all I had, dropped
to the ground, covered my face with hands as the
tribe started to punch, kick and spit. The beating
lasted an eternity of minutes then suddenly
stopped. I looked up puzzled to find a fine rain's
drizzle, the tribe's footsteps fizzling into the night
and a hooded figure holding a gun.


"don't shoot, I've got nothing, the tribe took all and ran"
"I don't want money, are you okay?"
"I'm fine, thanks for asking…and…scaring the tribe
away" I said lifting my bundle from where it lay.
"what's that?" she asked
"wood" I replied, she pulled down her hood, I saw the
question in her eyes,
"I turn them into things at my place"
"you're a sculptor" she asked completely disbelieving,
"listen" I said as the rain settled in, "I live a few streets
from here, let's get out of the weather, I'll show you, it's
over there…"

She saved my life, it was the least I could do. Back
at mine, I lit the gas fire and brewed two cups of
coffee, showed her sculptures in the workshop,
intricate figurines, replicas of buildings, door
knockers, wall clocks, the just-started other things;
the half-built model of South East with its tower
blocks like dark fists, threatening into sky.

"you made these?" she asked
"yes" I replied
"show me…I want to learn"
"sorry" I said, my voice level and stern "I don't teach, no
one knows this place is here, I only showed you 'cause
you helped back there"
"I saved your life".
I started to reply, realised she hadn't spoken any lie, if
she hadn't been passing by I'd be lying on the street,
"okay" I said after minutes of thinking, "but only a few
lessons, and only once a week…"

That night, I agreed to show all I knew about
wood-grain, shaving, joining, sawing, all I'd learnt
from mistakes and books.

For the first month I spoke a lot, she listened.
She'd only interrupt to ask questions with four-
worded sentences – that was patience-testing, like
"please say that again", "pass me the chisel". The
lessons were at night and always interrupted by
the traffic, chatter and laughter wafting in. By the
second month we'd found a rhythm around this.
Then I discovered the danger I was in.


    "Call me Lu" she said.


She was older than me, long hair, small nose,
deep dark brows. We talked about land where we
could find wood, grading the areas from bad to
good when she suggested I check the trees fallen
by her place on Croft St,


    "where's that?" I asked,
    "go past the closed factory, take the first right turn,
    through those old fields now covered with fern…,"
    "but…that's not safe ground" I said, "that's House of…"
    "Herne" she finished.

A shiver travelled the length of my spine. I sat
still, watched her watching me. I made for the
door, she sailed over the table and tackled me to
the floor.

"Listen" she said, her hand over my mouth, "I didn't tell
'cause there wasn't need to"
"why now" I screamed through a muffled mouth,
"I didn't mean to" she said, "it slipped out…I let my
guard down…thought we'd become friends"

An awkward silence that never seemed to end,
then

"okay" she said, "I'll get off your chest but think carefully
on what you do next"
"This block is owned by The Knights, they hurt people
like you"
"I know" she said, "that's why we work nights",
"but you guys are known as vicious brawlers"
"we are just like you Michael, we go to bed at night"
"but…The Knights won't hear that"
"listen" she said "if you can't handle this, we stop,
simple, but I think you like me and like working this
way. If you wish to continue, pass me a tool, I'll stay, if
not, we shake hands, I'll make my way…"
"damn, that's the most I've heard you say…"

So I pondered on it, looked from her outstretched hand, to the rest of my room, from the four dark corners to all four walls. From the scattered sandpapers, rustling like leaves, to the sheaves of curled shavings under the table. I looked to the ceiling where the light bulb dangling like one small sun swung back and forth and back and forth, I thought about all that could happen, all that could go wrong, shook my head a little…passed her a chisel.

I agreed on one condition, if ever The Knights grew suspicious, I'd end it. No questions, No explanations.

But we never got that far. Unknown to us, our movements were watched by The Knights, they'd kept a steady vigil on us, all the joining and sanding caused a lot of noise and there'd been more of it since Lu joined. By that lesson's end, we had two sacks full of scrap wood to recycle.

We stepped out wearing hoods, carrying one sack each and were instantly surrounded by a tribe of guys in hoods too.

"don't move" one said "we know all about you, trust me
some day you'll join this crew, what are you carrying?"
"just a sack of scrap wood"
"drop it on the ground"
"we're going to the scrap yard, what's this about?"
"just checking things, we like to know what goes in the
hood…who is that beside you?"
"cousin" I lied, my heart beating faster "she's from out of
town"
"let her talk, she seems to know her way around"


I watched in horror as they walked towards Lu,
almost shouted "watch out", I thought they'd
catch her surely, suddenly she lashed out with
her leg, threw the sack at one, uppercut the other,
vaulted their bodies and fled into the night. The
one who'd been speaking screamed in anger,
pulled back his hood and darted after Lu. I
caught a glimpse of his moon-lit face. I'd seen it
sprayed on every battle wall, he was a Knight of
Newtown. They called him Swift.

In all the land of Newtown toughened by steel
and grit, Swift was the fastest, most vicious Knight,
feared for his speed and terrible might, so when
he chased after Lu, I screamed "Hurry! don't stop
for a second!", till the three guys battered me
silent with fists. I stopped struggling after another
six kicks. Swift returned panting heavily. His
hands weren't bloody, so I knew he hadn't caught
her.

"Your Cousin? We'll see about that"

Dragged to the street light, Swift held a leather
pouch he opened. I gasped when I saw the card
clasped in his hand. There was a face on it, one
that I knew...

"Lulayan Issac," he spat, "42 Croft St, Herne House. You
hid our enemy, in our own land?!"
"She isn't like..."
"SILENCE! They're laughing at us right now, gotta do
something,
they'll take us for clowns"
"You are wrong..."

I was punched quiet by the men holding me
down. A moment passed then steadily Swift
began to laugh.

"I know...I'll challenge her to a duel."
"No, Swift, don't do that."

A duel is a fight. Two men meet and battle till one
falls, it's an aged tradition, old as stone walls but
these days duels weren't fought with swords but
guns, you fall, you don't get up.

"I'll call her out in front of her tribe, she'll have to
answer for honour and pride."
"What about this one?" the men holding me asked
"Let him go, catch him later, there's nothing he can do"

So Swift sent word through South-East streets, the
duel was set for Wednesday night and I couldn't
sleep, I hadn't heard from Lu. I wanted to believe
she wouldn't take his challenge, but peer pressure
makes us do foolish things, and I was afraid Lu
would fall victim, so I got dressed and crept out
towards the bridge, keeping all the way to the
shadows and side streets.

When I arrived everything was still, even the
traffic seemed to hold its breath, the few trees on
the pavement painted silver by the moon stood
still. No leaf moved. Then under the furthest one,
I saw something glint, saw the sleek design of
cold metal and a similar glimmer from across the
bridge. I ran into the centre, arms out stretched,
fingers splayed as if palms could bounce bullets.
Perched on the white lines, the light turned green,
the cars began flashing towards me. I screamed.
Over the roaring engines:

"Sorry Lu, Sorry Swift for bringing this between tribes,
I meant no harm, but bullets won't fix this, put the guns
down"

but they kept ducking and weaving, trying to
shoot around me. I screamed louder and louder
as the traffic's speed increased,

"Swift, Lu, bullets won't fix this…"

but they kept ducking…

"please, listen to me…"

And maybe it was something of the way I spoke,
or the moon bouncing from my chest, or the
dangerous scene of me begging between speeding
cars and light beams, but Lu's forehead cleared,
her frown disappeared, she lowered her gun and
Swift let his anger lift and laughed, his harsh voice
sand-papering past trees into the sky. Then both
of them shouted, arms out stretched, "Michael,
Michael get off the bridge!" I smiled relieved,
wondering who to meet, whose hand to shake
first, Lulayan or Swift, I turned quietly,


into a bus I did not see that charged into me,
knocked me through the ominous sky. Everything
went still. My body, lifted by the force of impact,
flew through the dark, over the rails, smashed the
river flowing below, with blood, like sap, seeping
into water, my skull splintered, my spine snapped.


Lu and Swift ran towards the rails, Swift stood
trembling, Lu choking wails, knowing I could not
have survived the sail, the hundred foot drop, the
churning waves. Swift lifted Lu who'd curled up
like wood shaving, sat her gently on the paving
and called the police.

Both neighbourhoods were quiet that week. In the days after I fell, both tribes gathered to pay respect to me. One minute's silence stretched from The House of Herne and The Knights of Newtown gathered in the cemetery, to solemn tribe members scattered in penitentiaries, who later that night lit a light each, a thousand candle fires linked by wind, blowing to forests and cities in between.

That night, I watched wind lift the leaves,
   wiped one tear from my eye
and stared through fog and rustling rain
   that came when Michael died,
I stared towards the Newtown lands,
   where shadowed towers rise.


The House of Herne and Newtown Knights
   like thugs caked in cotton
had walked the streets in perfect peace;
   for Michael we got on.
We watered flora, planted seeds,
   and pruned what was rotting.


As peace thrived between tribes, they talked
   of new alliances:
Like "KnightsHouse" or "HerneTown" whispered
   into the silences,
but I missed his workshops, his thoughts,
   all of his fantasies

I missed his soft ways, missed my friend
and missed his furrowed brow.
If I had walked away that night
he would be alive now.
The peace that reigned came from his death
I swore to guard it, vowed,


but there were odd things happening.
I tied my long hair back,
and turned to face the table piled
with files printed in black;
They told of days when flocks of birds
exploded from rucksacks.


How once, the bulbs in grey street lamps
all glowed a greenish blue,
and wild dogs gathered outside, sat
and howled by Michael's room.
I wondered what these things might mean
as Cox came running through.


"North of the city off Prime Street
a Knight too drunk to walk,
knocked one of us straight to the ground.
so now, the truce is off.
We must avenge, find where he lives…"
"No Cox", my hand raised up…

"We won't be starting careless wars
　　　　over liquor and lime.
My father left this throne to me
　　　　and I've made up my mind."
"If our men get no revenge
　　　　they'll rise against you, why…"


"If I see fists or one stone thrown
　　　　you'll wake to find me gone."
"You'll go?" Cox asked – his voice now high
　　　　"You'll leave all we have done?
You'll defect? For that…ant who died…"
　　　　I slapped Cox and he sprung.


We clashed mid-air, I scratched him, kicked
　　　　and held him to the floor,
"You know what Cox, do as you wish,
　　　　I won't rule any more,
I stood up, grabbed a hooded shirt
　　　　and crashed through the glass door


as Cox threatened to hunt me down
　　　　to send his hundred spies.
"No place to run, the Knights won't help"
　　　　you've no place left to hide."
Breathless, I ran to Newtown land
　　　　beneath the wind stormed sky.

Two days I hid in alleyways
        as Cox started the war.
Two Knights fell by Herne House knives,
        they fought back fast and raw
till chaos filled the streets again
        and pavements held their blood.


And as the fighters clashed above
        with sticks and stones and guns
I crawled through pipes and sewage drains,
        my hair grew thick with mud.
I surfaced by the corner and
        returned to Michael's shop


where everything was as it was
        even the lone light bulb,
from the scattered sand papers to
        the shelves built on the walls.
I thought of Michael's innocence
        and thought I hear him call.


Then saw my name scrawled on a box.
        I prised off the thin lid,
and found a note in Michael's hand
        addressed to... Lulay... Me?
"If you are reading this my friend,
        something's happened to me.

I don't know what the future holds
        but please go through this box.
And it will bring you peace of mind:
        do as the note instructs.
But Lu, you've got to leave South East
        till then it will not work."


I trembled in his quiet room.
        A soft breeze blew the leaves.
I searched the box, found a reed stick,
        a note, the first line reads…
"To make a simple wooden flute,
        These are the things you need"


Just then a voice: "ANYONE THERE?!
        swear I saw something move!"
They broke the door as I lashed out,
        I grabbed the box and tools,
and crashed through as they chased with dogs
        But I kept on the move.


And while I tunnelled underneath
        such wind storms blew the streets!
And still the strange things happening:
        the night roared with drumbeats
that echoed from dead factories
        that stood on South East Hills.

And still I ran, I only stopped
        to work on Michael's flute.
I'd break into abandoned homes
        to work the stick of wood.
My sweaty clothes choked all my skin
        I never once removed,


for, pressed between my chest and vest
        was Michael's careful note,
he thought he'd die by Swift or I
        yet, took the time and wrote?
Before my worries turned to cries
        I heard Cox getting close.


I ran, I reached the border walls
        and turned to face South East,
Its car fumes rose to kiss the clouds,
        the wind stormed thunderously,
The moon danced through its howling, lit
        the buildings brilliantly.


"But beauty lies in strangest things"
        Michael once said to me.
The flute was almost finished now,
        I'd carved out the mouth piece
and hollowed holes an inch apart,
        and washed the wood with spit

I reached the wall, my fingers raw,
     naked, tore at the stone.
Before I sailed over the top
     a Herne House voice bellowed
"This gun is pointed at your head,
     you betrayed us, your own!"


But just behind, a shadow rose,
     a Knight! I knew his face!
I watched as Swift pulled back his arm
     and pummelled Cox's face.
I lost my balance, falling back
     towards the ground with pace.


And as I fell, the oddest thing,
     a thick wind wrapped me whole,
I knew instinctively to blow,
     pulled out the flute, did so,
and all the rushing air and ground,
     and all of time turned slow


As sound escaped the flute I held
     grey wings grew out its holes
they flapped me gently to the ground
     and shrunk back through the holes.
I noticed the richness of soil
     how well plants here had grown.

I turned as moonlight slipped through clouds
        and licked the giant leaves,
I saw trees tall as stacked street lamps
        branches like tarpaulins
and petals thick as peeling paint
        they slow danced in night breeze.


The grounds rolled into valleys, cliffs,
        real mountains, no grey hills,
and rivers flowed as eyes could see
        did Michael plan all this?
When was he here? Why? How could he?
        Then I heard, loud and shrill


The same noises that left my flute
        they echoed through the dark;
a chorus blown from city slums
        came urgently and sharp
they had called out, they needed help
        and I had to go back.

The new moon rode high crowning the metropolis
shining: a queen on top of us,
and below the dark clouds where gathering
lightning was flashing and forces were amassing and


– battles broke, lives choked inside the battle smoke
and the wicked wind blew hard against our battle cloaks


      Gun cocked by the border walls,
I pulled back, struck Cox and he crumpled up,
the boys laughed "stamp down on his broken face"
but I ain't the type to kick a man down in his broken
state.


– Pick him up! March quick through the patchy fields,
that's a direct order son, leave behind the broken hills
– when we reach the city, leave the main streets and
battle fields


      rest you guns, shoot only if it's necessary
– detest death, you hear? even among enemies.

But The Knights didn't care, didn't listen to me
I was like a teacher and city was their playing fields.


Tower blocks, I tied Cox to a chair.
Here's a cup of water son, Listen, I don't care.
The battle's out of... shh, tss, Listen!
The battle's out of order, they massacre each other


Out there where the shadows glare,
– where the brittle bones clash and skin tissue tears
where the playgrounds boil and erupt with fear,
there's a dark fire burning, and a reckoning is coming.


Now Cox, I will let you go
if you go tell your men to live life slow
the foolish battle started with a cup of beer,
I gave you cup of water, we can end it here.


Cox spat in my face... "Die Swift,
the city is ours for the taking, as if
you pack of fools were threat to us,
we're gonna flush the city, turn you to dust."

        I pulled back, fist clenched, did he do that?
Did I just speak peace? Did he mean to do that?
Is that saliva dripping off my chin?
– I head-butt, head-crush, till he toppled clean,


– a couple men told me Cox was dangerous
once burned a house down 'cause the girl said leave
            saw a man frown, and crushed his knees
            wanted to save the city, and I didn't need this.


*(Sound of flutes playing.)*


The door was hammered, the men rushed in, "Swift
the House of Herne are taking over Newtown streets
– they're looting the schools, the shops, the banks,
chemists
and setting fire to the alleys, suffocating our men,
I'm telling you when we let scum run free,
when we let them…" shhhs, listen


*(Sound of flutes playing.)*


"what's that?" they asked. Light flashed.


*(Sound of flutes playing.)*

Sound like horns, a chorus of flutes
must be hundreds of them, gathered…I'm going to look,
– stay here, watch Cox, he's dumb as he looks
if he stirs, knock him unconscious or give him a book,


That was it, that was me, straight out the door
and I'd never seen South East battered before.
Shattered before, broken and torn, scattered before
with traffic lights rammed through the windows of stores


pipes burst, water gushing out of it, more
– cars on fire / tyres slashed, windows and doors
– crashed, the glass splintering, lights flickering on.
From the bottom of the street came a riotous roar


I ducked as rocks flew / over and tore through /
another tribe coming running out of a door.
Walls crashed, gas flamed into the night,
I tumbled in the street as a tower of smoke roared


into a corner, we washed last week
cleared its rubble planting trees last week. Funny
how little things never mattered before,
but as the little tree fried, I was begging for pause,

I'm telling you, war leaves walls battered and torn
but the true victims, usually: the weak and the poor.


Herne House think that the battle is won,
– but this is South East, I'm Swift, I am the law. Stand UP!
         Knee deep in debris, I climbed up.
Had to find the men, had to tell 'em It's Time, STOP!
Had to the find the leaders before my time's up.
Had to find those horns, they make time stop.


         Malcolm Street, riddle with heat.
Saw an old lady crying and I gave her some keys
– Take this, a car's parked on Middleton Lane
find your friends, stay together, the city is insane.


         Smith Road, was glowing like gold
saw a church like a furnace, burning, splitting the road
– in half, I doubled back, as the thunder clapped
after lightning, the sky turned a darker black.


– Mine Street, hidden by the crumbling church, I saw
many shadows tunnelling through broken stalls,
– some crawled. Each, holding something fragile and small,
a figure by a door waving, beckoning them.

I grabbed from the rubble, thin sticks and I turned
– through the door, up stairs / I followed them up
– flights of stairs, sixth floor, there're twenty of us
– reached the roof, top floor / they're ready to jump.
– they're ready to jump – they're ready to jump –
– they're ready to jump – they're ready to jump –


STOP!


       I know the city is on fire,
I know that some nights the smog clogs and makes you
tired
foul play rise each month, there's gunfire
and the old folks call it the funeral pyre


– you burn – But the city's got a warmer side
– step from the edge, come, hear about the winter's ride
       how stone hills double up as water slides
and in the summer, steel works shine with pride


– don't jump! – don't jump! –

"Don't listen to him, you've seen this before,
        hold the flute, blow through, go tumbling, fall
and wings will lift you to the border walls" –
Said a voice behind me… Lulayan What?!


Didn't I see you fall over a wall?
You're back in the city and you're killing them all.
– "Shut up Swift! I'm not doing this it's Michael"
He died – "Yeah, I'm not sure any more.


– besides, the city is aflame tonight.
and you men, you never know when to fold or fight"


        Lulay snapped her fingers and they turned to
dive,
I screamed NO! and stopped when I heard it rise:
        The chorus of horns and the slow of time
– as twenty of them flew through the stormy skies.


*(Sound of flutes playing.)*


        Lulayan Issac, gimme that flute!
"No, it's mine." You must, or I'll take it from you.
"Come on and try" She said, a glint in her eyes
        we tussled and the girl fought wicked and wild

– as the storm grew angry, shook the skies
/ the clouds broke, rain drops hard as ice
– struck our eyes and we turned temporarily blind.


"Swift stop, there's no need to fight,
let's leave this roof top, its bucketing down
come close, hold my hand, edge of the roof
ready?        I'm blowing the flute…"


*(Sound of flutes playing constantly now.)*


We soared over South East
– on the ground, I thought the battle was the wildest.
– But up there, getting lashed by the bullets of rain,
– the wind whipping ridiculous, stars twinkling strange


I saw South East for what it was,
The fires raging, the concrete burned
      walls crumbling, lights flickering off
– and battles scattering right through the slums


from play grounds right to the churches steeped
      courtyards, squares and factories
soot stained and dust scorched, the fire breathed
      and our people crumbled to their knees

every nook, every cranny, every corner, every alley
the flames and the furnace, the rage was tumultuous
– like volcanoes rumbling, it would soon erupt
– like volcanoes rumbling, it would soon erupt.
like a volcano, South East erupts!

I woke up in a forest. The waves must have spat
me outside the city. All I recalled was a flash, my
body lifted off the bridge, the splash, pain, then
nothing. I lay half sunk in water and struggled
to remember my own name. Whatever it was,
something else was strange, I felt different. I
threw up gobs of water. The pebbles and sharp
stones pierced my skin, I gasped and felt the
ground soften beneath! I sneezed, the breeze
stilled. I coughed, the river stopped. I raised a
hand, a drop fell, splashed the still water and
rippled along the bank, tickling the reeds. But I
felt it flowing inside me, through muscle, veins,
then pipes, sewers, drains, I felt the heat of a
boiling city, and South East came flooding back,
memories of Swift, Lulayan, and the bridge.
Above, the sky thundered four times and I sensed
the storm's size coming for South East.

I ran through the forest and saw it once held a great city. The roots of trees had tangled with breeze blocks and old iron. Shattered glass had grown into trees and they glittered like brittle stars amongst leaf. There were fallen statues dressed in shrubbery, branches out of windows where oaks had grown through floorboards and soil had swallowed houses whole, street after street, block after block. I closed my eyes and this forest spoke to me: running river water, hidden streams and pools. I hiked on till I'd reached the city, a plan had formed. Lu had to see the forest.

I found a sharp stone, carved a reed flute, chanted the forest wind through the wood, blew, and lifted to where Herne House stood, I landed. Glass shattered and from the shadows, Lu hit the cobbled stones and dashed past as a man cursed her, threatening with spies. Whatever needed doing, I had to do fast.

Lu made for Newtown, I was all she knew so thought she'd make for my workshop and room. I arrived first, left notes to build a flute and spent the days after running the city through as battle broke between Knights and Herne House.

I gave out boxes and half-built flutes in attics,
basements, crypts, roofs, alleys, even waited in
the gloom for any I thought might help the battles
cool.


The city boiled with smoke and fire and Lulayan
did as I thought she'd do: reached the border
walls, touched the forest floor, saw there was
something worth fighting for and returned to help
those trapped in the city.


I expected her, waited in the fields, hid in the
bushes, begged the wind's calm. As it dropped,
they landed, I walked towards them. Hundreds,
gathered, crouched around Lu, listening as she
talked the happenings through.


"I know you all say the same thing
        all found a box or flute,
all say why we are gathered here
        are mysteries to you.
And though I don't know what to do,
        I know a thing or two."


"The instructions to build the flute
        came from my friend who died."

Lu…

"Just hold a second, young man, now
        the flute means we can glide…"

Lu…it's me, it's Michael.

She turned, screamed, fell down and Swift?!…
helped her to her feet.

"You di…we saw you fall off the bridge.
        Where've you come from?
are you doing this?

  "Lu, I don't know how I'm here, why skies are
  turning or how the flutes work, I just know we
  are wasting time. Our city will fall tonight. A
  storm is coming. Swift, please bring the people
  here, but as you march out set everything to
  burn. Lu, can I lead the tribe of flutes?"

Lu looked at Swift who shrugged and turned from
me.

"Michael is your friend, what do you think?"

"Promise you'll be back..." She asked. I nodded and Lu yelled

"They're yours to command, do as you wish."


"Fan out. Go South and West, a quarter to the East, those left come North with me. Climb the border walls, wait for my signal. Swift, I'll watch for you. Right, move quick."


Lu watched as the flute tribe stood beside each other and blew their flutes high. There rose a clamour, a chorus of such force, that all the wind paused, and all the storm sighed and in the brief stillness, we entered the sky.


The storm attacked, thrashed us aside and whipped river water from the wide banks, down the narrow drains, burst the city mains, till South East flooded, never to dry again.


Below, Lu and Swift had gathered both their tribes, who pushed, bullied, till all the folks had climbed the hills of South East, and turned to watch the tide drown the flaming city, never to burn again.

Block after block, shook at their base, shuddered
as wet soil sucked in trains, swallowed whole
streets; such was the damage, roads couldn't be
built again.

And as fires struggled, as water drowned, as earth
sucked the city, I called the wind down, I gave up
my breath, took the tempest in, called the flute
tribe, "Now, together blow" and all the sounds
united, through the great storm struck the high
towers, turned them to low plains so the city's
stench, would never blow again.

We watched spires twist, heard fires hiss, saw
bridge after road after courtyard all sink.
Newspapers, boxes, clothes, sheets, bowls and
islands of waste dipped below. The last roof
beam slipped beneath the water. The city was
destroyed, utterly and grim.

I collapsed, I fell. I recall the rush of air, but woke
on the ground where a fight had begun.

"Behind you", I shouted. "There's a forest filled with homes, they're old but there're houses, grown into trees, ask Lulayan Issac, she knows what I have seen. Lu nodded swiftly, "Over the wall, you'll see…"

And all the people gathered on South East's hills turned towards the borders, lost, confused but free, eyes blazing like candles lit.

And all candles are cousins of the sun. The moon plays foster mother. The waters swear always to refelct her light. Dust is daughter to these givers of life, all grandmother'd by nature holding tight, in this patch-work order, this unclear night, we all are prodigal sons. We alone journey to spirit city, but earth remains our home.

BLACK T-SHIRT COLLECTION

*Black T-shirt Collection* was first performed at Unity Theatre, Liverpool on 9 March 2012.

*Written and performed by* Inua Ellams
*Directed by* Thierry Lawson
*Designed by* Michael Vale
*Lighting Design by* Michael Nabarro
*Sound Design by* Emma Laxton

In chronological order, thanks to:

James T. Kirk, Jean-Luc Picard, Benjamin Sisko, Kathryn Janeway, Krystle Lai, Kate McGrath, Louise Blackwell, Christina Elliot, NPR's Planet Money Podcast Team: Jacob Goldstein, Alex Bloomberg, Adam Davidson, Hannah Jaffe Walsh, Thierry Lawson, Ed Collier, Paul Warwick, Alan Ryvet, Nii Parkes, Nina Steiger, Kayo Chingonyi, Ore Disu, Samuel Sabo, Felicia Okoye, Danella Officer, Nadia Latif, Sabrina Mafhous, Simon Block, Frances Poet, Shiui Weng, Nick Starr, Sebastian 'Bash' Born, Gabbi Wong, Dipo Salimonu, James Baldwin, Roz Wynn, Ed Errington & the other angel-feathered folk at Fuel, Vicki Heathcock, Michael Vale, Michael Nabarro, Michael Alebiosu, Danielle Evans, Connie Abbe, Gabrielle Smith, Franklyn Rodgers, Charlotte Wilkinson, Lupe Fiasco, Estabrak Al-Ansari, Shehab El-Tawil, Martin Roberts and the ever relentless Ellams.

Dedicated to the bridge-builders of our time
& to Josh & Musa. (Just talk. Please.)

Let me begin again, I say, as the bar blurs
invisible, its volume reduced to the merest
suggestion of others and it's just us spotlit
in the black womb-like silence of theatre
and your question themes the play; let me
begin again: I went to church last Sunday.

The pastor preached: put not your faith in
man who only is good as his next breath;
align your faith with he who gives breath.
Here I stutter, my answer splintering like
fragments of bone against the mud soil
of memory. Moments before, I recalled

the call to prayer: In the Name of Allah
Most Gracious, Most Merciful – the slow
unfurling Imam's son's voice as dusk
touched the courtyard, the dust settling,
the sun solemnly bowed on the horizon –
thin as a prayer mat – and the gathered
performing ablutions: Bismillah, they say,
washing hands, mouths, nostrils, faces,
arms, head, ears, feet, kneeling to pray
Allah Is Great, God Is Great, they say.

You counter with airplanes, fireballs,
towers falling; stop your rant with
the first fireman to die, his skull caved
by a jumper from the 51st floor fleeing
flames. In the name of Allah, Gracious,
Great, Merciful this was done, you say.

I mention Amazing Grace, how sweet
the choir leader swayed in white robes,
eyes closed, humming southern baptist
hymn hypnotic, sailing congregations
to the oceanic depth whence his tears:
wide and sure as waves ride back and
forth that everything would be all right.

You rejected faith again, describing Jos,
Nigeria, the girl watching flat amongst
tall grass: the squad of Christian men
who hold her mother down as another
swings down with a machete, down as
sunlight skates the blade's edge, down,
the last swing, the fragments of bone
and there are screams no more.

There's blood in the drama of Men and
Gods, you say: rivers of it flow through
our wounded earth, gush from scripts
in houses of worship and act after act
aren't all stained? except the audience?
the secular astray? You gesture toward
those seated in darkness who gawk as we
squabble on stage; Aren't they the ones
the light beyond will touch unbloodied?
who will die hands clean?

… Let me begin again, I say, I went to
church/the pastor preached/faith/man
/breath/… I stutter, the bar blurs back
to life, words fall against your ears.

'For, while the tale of how we suffer, and how we are delighted, and how we may triumph is never new, it always must be heard. There isn't any other tale to tell, it's the only light we've got in all this darkness.'
**James Baldwin,** *Sonny's Blues*

PART 1 //

*Sound –*

*A man moving around in darkness.*

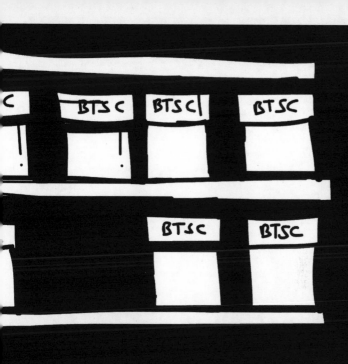

Matthew is struck dumb by the brightness on the landing; he squints, his eyes like tadpoles scurry from the light, he tries to hide behind the box as if he were small enough – **Welcome** – Ayah, the sister says – **We knew you'd come, come to the parlour, I've been waiting, so has Mum –**

He trembles in the living room's stifling darkness and nothing's changed since the wake, weeks ago. Night squeezes through slits in the curtain, she says nothing but Halima, the mother, she is sat on the left. At the far end, a floor lamp is lit. Its low glow licks the rich thick carpet and flowers drooping in the humid heat. Ayah, the sister, takes her chair and begins:

**– So, I heard you punched the pastor on Sunday? He's fine, think you fractured his jaw, but you've done it this time, some cracks don't heal? Why'd you do that to him? Eh? Matthew, They say you want to close the shop? It's all you've got since... –**

Her tongue fails her, mouth suddenly dry and Matthew finishes – **since Muhammed died?** – Ayah curls up, knees to her chest. There's nothing save her muffled sobbing, just breath and darkness. Across the room her mother, Halima, who'd spoken not a word, lifts her head lightly like a morning mist, lifts, dignified, the way queens do, whispers – **Tell me how he died. Tell me how he died. TELL ME HOW MY SON DIED, YOU BASTARD BOY, YOU WILL KILL ME IN THIS HOUSE! YOU WILL KILL ME O! Tell me how my son –**

**– He loved you –** Ayah says as Halima, her mother cries – **You were his favourite story to tell, he'd stop board meetings, bank managers, bar tenders, lean over, order that stupid drink of Scottish Scotch and Ribena, lean forward and say 'It all started with him you know' –** Muhammed would say 'Way back when we were boys, I ran with some bastard guys eh! Naija's answer to John Travolta! Greased back hair, tight black jeans, trying to enter clubs or smoking, watching girls. All the small boys wanted to be like us you know, so we'd send them on impossible tasks "Sssss! Aeyssss! Small boy, come here. Take this 5 Naira, go to the shop, buy me 2 fried fish, 3 bottles of coke, 1 Fanta, 6 packs of cabin biscuits, 3 Guinness, 2 Moimoi, 7 Tomtoms and 9, no 10, 11…20 chewing sticks. Oya GO! Ayessss! I want my change O!" Impossible! Anyway, it was Matthew's turn and Zebra Santana, that was his nickname, don't ask, Zebra Santana sent him. But Matthew did what we hated most, returned empty handed, sniffing, crying as if all the desert dust had blown into his eyes. Zebra Santana just runs, kicks him in his chest, Matthew lands and bounces in the sand, doesn't move. I go, punch Santana to the ground, then "Matthew, bro you OK?" And Matthew, he unfurls, slow, like a dust flower, except, he is looking at his black shirt. Santana's footprint: stamped on his chest; perfect stone crystals glinting in the grooves. Bro looks at me with his little, big eyes, says "Let's go home" I lift him and he says to mum 'D'you have some black cloth?' and copied the footprint pattern from the shirt. Next day we set up shop. Zebra Santana was the first customer after he apologised. We sold 30 shirts in 2 days and that was it! Black T-shirt Collection, thank you, Bob's your uncle, gimme the cash, over and out! All started with him you know!' **– He loved you –** Ayah says **– Now you want to dismantle his life's work? –**

So this is about Muhammed. Musaddiq Zango, walking home from work, was stopped by a group of Christian men, vexed at a beheading of their brethren in the city of Kano, north of where they stood. They asked Musaddiq what he thought of this. He replied it wasn't his business and tried to walk away. Muhammed was twelve, Ayah was five when their father, Musaddiq, Halima's husband died. Halima banned religion from her house. One month passed and Halima returns with Matthew from a children's home **– Kids, this is your brother –** They wished to fill the void Musaddiq left with someone to look after, one who needed love. This was unheard of at the time, a

Christian boy fostered in a Muslim house. Matthew was just seven, he clenched the hem of Halima's wrapper, a slow breeze twirled a loose dangling thread, he snapped it off. Muhammed smiled **– Would you like to be my friend? –** his arm stretched out like an olive branch.

They grew tight after that, inseparable friends of scuffed knees and stone-throwing-sand-magic, salt of the earth type of childhood living in Jos, Plateau State, Nigeria. When violence broke out between Muslims and Christians with casualties reported on both sides, Halima tried to hide the kids from it. Still some days, Muhammed returned with bruised fists battling those who'd tease his foster brother at school. Muhammed had a sense of what was right and wrong and tried to guard Matthew from the world in-between. Most fights they'd lose; slammed against a wall, Muhammed's arms swinging out at the world, Matthew down low, raining in kicks. The kids would snatch Matthew, press him to the ground and pour sand across his nose and mouth, chanting 'Onward Christian Soldier'. Matthew'd look forlorn and helpless at Muhammed and stir such holy anger in him, he'd burst through those holding him back and attack: a wild animal scratching this way, that, to collapse on the ground by Matthew. They'd hold each other there, bruised, covered in dust, sand in their hair. Something impossible was forged there, down on the ground: an absolute trust that whatever else life could thrust at them, they'd face it together. This was unspoken between the boys, this complete, fight formed, dust-ridden-trust.

They'd spend hours together, purposely get lost in fields and not speak a single word. They loved the silence that was choked by others: Halima's brothers who said this was wrong, teachers at school, pastors and imams. They'd splash about naked in the lukewarm streams, or tag team through Super Mario video games. One afternoon in mango season, the sun splashing through the canopy of leaves, they sat under a mango tree and ate every fruit that fell. They got very sick, Halima couldn't explain it and the boys refused to tell. It hurt more than most fights they'd lost but getting beaten was never any fun and after Santana and the Black T-shirt stall, Muhammed thought he could end it all: **– Simple Matthew, if they like us, they won't fight us, and they'll pay us at the same time! You make shirts, I'll talk to them –** Matthew found a sewing machine, an old Singer one tossed in a skip, and taught himself the ins and outs of it. When the treadle broke, he used a drain grate, when the treadle belt broke, he used his own belt, stitching letters cut out of felt; lyrics of songs or playground rhymes, especially rude ones. It worked. Enemies would pause mid-fight, fold up their arms and ask sheepishly **– erm…where'd you get that –** and orders came thick and fast.

A nightclub. Eight years after that, the boys have blossomed to beautiful black men. Matthew is quiet, a typical artist, T-shirt designer, all pencils and pens; Muhammed is charismatic, the salesman. Print by print, stitch by stitch, nightclubs, markets, hawking their tees – free ones to kids and celebrities. A rapper wore one on the cover of an album and that was it, money, rolling in. Limited edition runs of all prints, once they sold out, never again. Their fastest selling shirt was a simple one; Matthew had drawn a white lake such that the black of the shirt seemed like oil spilling into waves. On the back of the shirt he'd written 'Dear Shell, Water No Get Enemy' – lyrics from the Fela Kuti song that everyone loved, its gentle rhythms like waves to ear. Beneath the writing he'd left a space so who bought the shirt could sign their name and they'd wear these T-shirt letters to protests and campaigns against the hell Shell caused. But, they played wild with those shirts, some held together by wooden pins, some strung to wear just once, some of long thin detachable sleeves, some stitched entirely of leaves **– Ayah, remember those crazy things? –** Matthew wants to ask her, still frozen in the gloom, he imagines a smile might ghost Ayah's lips… He doesn't speak. Fingertips grip the white box, shoulders droop deep, feet shuffle on the carpet. He recalls when they sold their ten thousandth shirt.

A nightclub. They celebrate: huge party! Half of Jos city come their way, the journalists, stylists, competitors, all cramped in the bowel of the nightclub, floors slippery wet with hot sweat and Guinness, strobe lights flickering the rhythmic and sizzling stretch of hot flesh, all who got to witness that night said that they were kings!

Halfway through, Muhammed disappears. Matthew asks his girlfriend Zuki **– Where's my bro? –** And follows her jerking thumb down to the bathroom. Muhammed is by the sink, kissing a man.

The door bursts open, a journalist behind screams when he sees this **– Matthew grab him! –** Matt nabs him by his collar, slams the door shut **– Abomination! You'll make my career, when my editors hear you are a fucker of men, you'll be lynched! –** Muhammed's friend bolts out the door. Bass thumps the weak floorboards. Dust falls off the cheap peeling plaster. Matthew, Muhammed and the journalist stand still. Death fills the room. Muhammed offers the journalist cash, who throws his head back, laughing, cackling **– No amount of money will save your life –** Muhammed leans forward, strikes him to the ground. Matthew's eyes narrow in the dirty mirror. The journalist's cries shatter his nerves. The sick sound of fists pounding flesh. Matthew and Muhammed climb out the window as the journalist rises off the floor. Outside, they collapse against the cold walls.

**– Matthew –** Muhammed speaks **– It's over, I'm done, you know what happens to people like… This is Naija. There's no place to hide. They'll kill me, burn our house down… I have to run. Now, look after mum and // I'm coming –** Matthew says, his voice sudden, brave as blood **– Different city, different country, different world, new shop. // But we've built so much, you can stay here and // No, you can't go on your own, it'll be good for us and the business Muhammed, listen… Listen! We'll be fine. Let me handle this one, we get orders from Cairo, I know someone, let's go eh? That city sucks up Africans like Zuki sucks dick –** Matthew says, inappropriate, warmth in his voice. Muhammed melts with Matthew's kindness. Doesn't trust his voice, just hugs his foster brother, thankful that the cover of darkness hides his tears: two slim streams in the shadow of the club **– Few hours –** Matthew says **– then we disappear.**

*Sound –*

*Flight.*

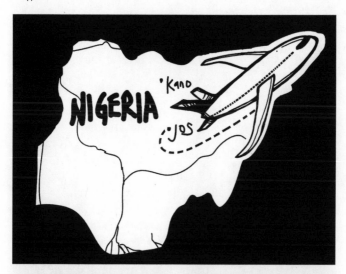

Sheikh Farhat is 56 and thinks he has seen everything. He presents a stern countenance and hides his good humour and weak chin beneath a thick beard that most people see through. He is too quick to smile and the Egyptian sun twinkles his eyes too much. He has lost one son, so, he is partial to lost boys wandering the cobbled-stone alleys and old architecture of Khan el-Khalili, Cairo's biggest market. He is a carpet seller here and loves the flow of money, the back and forth of haggling, the smell of all currencies, says his finger holds the pulse of the world; he loves what he does with an unmatched passion; he is in charge of two streets, this one and the next. He knows them intimately, Warsan's stall of rare spices, the young men who play backgammon all day. The conmen with tacky souvenirs for the British, how slips of the Khamsin, the desert wind, twirls thin scarves Masuma sells and Mahmoud, further back who snoozes all day jumps when sand grains twang his instruments **– Voice of an angel –** Farhat murmurs **– You should hear his call to prayer –** Farhat sits cross-legged among his carpets to watch his world walk by.

**– MMM –** he nods, a cousin passes by **– MMM!! –** he smiles at a young lady **– MMM? –** he frowns at two black men, boys to his eyes. Faces unwashed, haven't slept for nights. The sheikh can tell by how the young one clutching a white box to his chest, sways, almost falls with each step. He stares as they walk up to him and the older one speaks **– Sheikh Farhat? they say you are a kind man? –**

**– MMM They lied! –** Farhat replies **– D'you have place we can stay? We will bring good business. // What Kinda? –** Farhat asks **– T-shirts –** He adds as the sheikh begins to laugh **– but a different kind eh? Just give us a chance. // You have something I can see? –** The younger one lifts a black shirt from the box into Farhat's hands. There's an old leaf spread out like a palm print on its chest. It's held in place by thin black thread. Farhat holds the T-shirt close to his chest. A gust of the Khamsin thrusts through his stall and the dried leaf disintegrates to dust. **– You have name for this? –** Farhat asks **– Yes –** says Matthew **– It's called A Week's Work –** The sheikh, he excuses himself, says something's in his eye, a speck of leaf, and retreats into his stall. **– A Week's Work? –** asks the older one, the young one shrugs, **– No! It's good, name them all –** Farhat returns and the older one speaks **– We have others, better ones –** Farhat studies their faces intently **– OK –** he says **– rest tonight, wash. Tomorrow, new week, you start work. Name? // I'm Matthew, this is Muhammed –** Later that night, Matthew tries Halima, tapping her number into a payphone, but each time he gets an engaged tone.

Two months pass. Business starts slow. 'Matt & Mo' as the boys are now known by street kids who clatter past the patterned stone walls, 'Matt & Mo' know Cairo like it gave them backbones. Sales are slow, but Farhat is confident, he invested money, most of it his own **– S'OK, Nigeria wasn't built in a day –** Muhammed laughs into his cup of mint tea, spilling some on Matthew **– Sss! Muhammed watch it now // Sorry, how's it going eh? // Well, I have an idea –** he says, beckoning Muhammed near. Farhat laughs too and conjures back the night the boys told a treacherous flight to Sudan, a smuggler who got them quickly into Egypt, four days walking the desert terrain and **– here we are –** Muhammed finished. **– But why did you leave? –** Muhammed had a sudden coughing fit and stood out in the cold, Matthew at his side. Returning, they asked if they could rest. Farhat bowed low **– Allah and the Khamsin know best –** he said **– tomorrow! –** He chose a compact stall stacked with white boxes packed with black shirts. Matthew set to work sketching out ideas, Muhammed made friends in Khan el-Khalili **– Business is slow, first thing, get noticed –** Muhammed advised **– I've just the thing –** said Matthew, mischief in his eyes.

Now, the street kids of el-Khalili are fast, I mean The-Khamsin-fast, have almost a 6th sense whereabouts a person's wallet, purse or camera hides; can estimate exactly how much distraction is needed to snatch, leaving tourists surprised at their speed. Their natural enemies: police, dark sunglasses, truncheons at their side.

Bakari was the slowest of the fastest street kids, caught at least once every single week. It's Thursday, the heat is high. Bakari partners with a fake whirling dervish, a guy who copies the Sufi spinning dance. A Sudanese woman drops her bag to clap, and when the shout goes up, Bakari is out fast, scattering past stalls of dried seeds, running low. An officer, hot on his heels closes in, inches from Bakari's shirt. He stretches further, grabs a fistful, yanks, and the back of Bakari's black shirt is in his hand; Bakari rapidly fading in the distance. The market erupts in laughter. He tries to feign anger, but leans against the wall, hugging his sides **– Who did this? Where this come from? –** they point out the black shirt stall **– You did this? –** Matthew nods **– Good work, good work, what you call it? // The... Back-a-rip? // His name! Bakari! Clever, good! So. You make shirt for anyone? // Yes –** Matthew replies **– You make for...us? // Yes –** Matthew smiles, spreads his hands along the counter **– Tell me about yourself –** Over his shoulder Muhammed twirls the fake whirling dervish. They turn down a side street, quiet as mice. Matthew hadn't broached his sexuality, hoped Muhammed would when he felt comfortable. This went unspoken between the boys. Matthew stares after them, squints into the gloom **– Matthew? –** Farhat calls **– You have customer // Matthew –** Ayah calls **– Listen to mother. Matthew? Matthew! Mum is talking to you –**

Matthew shakes off the memory, blinks, breathes and slowly returns to Nigeria. The living room's gloom is thick as guilt, it weighs on his shoulders, it suffocates him **– You left so quickly –** Halima says **– Business opportunity. Good one. Cairo –** Matthew speaks finally **– That not all is it Matthew? –** Ayah says **– You should have told us. We were worried, we didn't hear for months! Years! You return. Muhammed's in a box...this is all you are going to say? //** Matthew stays silent, he licks his lips, thirsty, but won't ask for water **– So, are you happy? –**

asks Halima from the dark **– Was it worth it? –** Matthew, shakes his head from side to side, lifts his face up, sucks back tears. The room swims, he shuts his eyes and tries to conjure Muhammed's face, he thinks of one eve in Cairo, waiting for Muhammed to arrive.

**– Matthew? –** Farhat asks **– Business going well? What is wrong? // Ahh, it's not enough! –** Matthew speaks into the coming dusk that strides across the sky, crouches on the buildings, a thousand lights in el-Khalilli glow. They don't live here anymore. Matthew misses it. 18 months since they first arrived and the Black T-shirt business is alive! Their shirts are sought after by high-street shops whose staff come all the way here to the Khan. Muhammed's hired staff to meet their demands. They own six stalls now scattered through the market and Matthew's light touch humbles everyone: limited edition calligraphic writings of Qur'ānic verses or Rumi's poems. Anti-government icons, edges sharp as blades, yet supple as water. For the brave ones, bold statements in English and in Arabic: flower-like inscriptions that seem aflame; they blaze in the eyes of the Cairo youth. Their clientele go from the street kids to rich offspring of Egypt's elite who ask 'Matt & Mo' to parties thrown for what reasons they conjure, their job is to come with T-shirts stitched for the night's wild soul. Typically, those nights, Matthew doesn't go, prefers to stay alone in the Zamalek district, in the low-lit apartment they'd come to call home. Now and then Matthew calls Halima, but the line had gone from engaged to dead. He'd stay hunched over, white sheets about him, sketching ideas quick as they come; his shelves are lined with art books, couple on sculpture, in height order they stand up tall, like an installation he curates these walls, flicks through them daily, learns from them all.

He gets up and walks to Muhammed's room. In contrast, it looks like the Khamsin hit it. T-shirts strewn, this way, that. Towels dangle from hangers half-damp, half-dragged across the carpet through plates of food. Matthew laughs to himself. On Muhammed's shelf: photographs of his new Egyptian friends. Matthew sits on the bed and flicks through. There's one photograph of Halima, Muhammed and Ayah – **I'm not in it, so I must have snapped –** Matthew thinks and remembers the day after that. They had learnt about genetics at school, in the kitchen where Halima stood, Matthew asked nervously – **Where're my parents? –** Halima, transformed to a thing of stillness, turned, walked to him and sat down – **Matthew I knew this day would come. Your parents moved from the village you were born and the children's home lost track of them. They loved you, but couldn't feed you, couldn't afford to send you to school, so I thought**

**I could help. I've done alright eh?** – Matthew didn't answer. He walked to Halima, hugged her tightly and left the room. The next day he went round to the village and gave every penny he'd saved from the shirts. The villagers, they thanked him endlessly. Mothers clutched their young and hugged him, fathers shook his hand and Matthew felt something he'd never felt before and every month after returned when he could to give as much as he could. In Cairo, a dark shirt falls on the lamp tainting the light that filters through. Matthew sits on the edge of the mattress, lost in his thoughts, bathed in blue. Muhammed staggers in laughing from the party, Matthew stands up – **Bro, it's not enough. // Eh?** – Muhammed says sobering up – **It's not enough, we need to expand and make more money! You should talk to that man you know // Aha? What are we doing with all the cash? We make more than we spend and you give yours to those crazy kids anyway. Why do you do that Matthew? They steal more in a week than we make in a month! We can manage this size, let's not get too big O! // But businesses grow, otherwise they get stagnant, Muhammed you know this, just go and ask him. Do this small thing for me, I left Naija for you // For me?... OK, I'll ask him** –

Matthew waits as the dusk strides low and a thousand lights in el-Khalilli glow – **Farhat, he went hours ago, where can he be? // Matthew, Muhammed tries to protect you, there isn't a dishonest drop in his blood. If he says he will come, he will come. Ah, here he is!** – Muhammed embraces Sheikh Farhat, asking of his family. Matthew interrupts – **How did it go? // Are you sure Matthew, this is what you want? OK, I spoke to him, it is done** –

He had spoken with Hassan Winter in Cairo, a French-speaking / PR / publicist / stylist / maestro with a Moroccan-Clark-Kent-in-a-tux thing going for him, thick-frame glasses, he blinked slowly when he talked. He liked women, Muhammed discovered when they talked about European markets **– Matthew –** Hassan said **– I'll make you a star –** arms around them both, his breath of pine trees and toothpaste. He planned everything; trips to six trade shows: 'Fashion' in Helsinki, 'CIEN X CIEN' in Madrid, 'Zoom' in Paris, 'Bread & Butter' in Berlin, tiny one in Florence and a big one in London. Every single shirt would come from Cairo, Matthew hired kids off el-Khalili streets and trained them to copy the simplest designs. Farhat, now quality manager, set to work designing production lines. A hive of activity buzzed in Cairo, Matthew at its centre, Muhammed at his side. At trade shows, a few of the street kids would act out Bakari's back-a-rip trick and when screaming stopped and security arrived, they'd point out the Black T-shirt stall. It worked, everyone flocked to the boys. Buyers, romanced by the roughness of it all, bought Matthew's designs to sell at stores in Amsterdam, Lisbon, Düsseldorf, Minsk, Brussels, Athens, London and more, Farhat called to complain how demand was too great for the boys to match, he laughed as he spoke and Matthew replied **– It's all in a week's work.**

A month later, the boys are back in Cairo, sitting in a café, sipping mint tea and Farhat walks in, a newspaper in his hands **– What is this? –** a frown scars his face. The headline reads of mass graves in Jos, a new one discovered, four hundred killed and goes on to detail the history of the conflict. Farhat sits, confused and shocked **– But You 'Matthew', You 'Muhammed' Go back! Show them friendship work, they kill their brothers! // It's not easy, we –** Matthew stops **– Farhat –** says Muhammed **– we can't return but please don't ask us why –** Farhat leaves not angry but hurt, for he'd come to think of the boys as sons. That night, Muhammed tries Ayah's workplace. The phonecall had been a long time coming. Matthew suggested it months ago, but Muhammed, fearing what she might think, begged Matthew **– bro, few more weeks. I'm just not…I dunno…let me think –** A choir of questions choked their throats. What happened to the journalist? When news broke, how had Ayah and Halima coped? Were they questioned by police? Arrested? Lashed? At work, was Halima ever attacked? Was the house burned down? Were they beaten? Were they stoned? Muhammed holds the handset close as Matthew dials the number. They sit, silence about them stiff and coiled in quiet, listening for the tone, the earpiece cupped between both palms **– The number you are calling is out of order, please try again later –** Muhammed heaves a sigh of relief, instantly followed by fear that grows within the hour, hardens every day. They try every week, nothing ever changes, same message every second, every time they call and after six months the boys give up and seek new ways to reach them.

A whole year had passed since the trade fairs; Hassan suggests a move to London for the client base there grows bigger by the week. Farhat, thinks this a fine idea and makes for them a parting gift of a carpet, hand stitched with early designs, the first ones from the months they'd arrived penniless in Cairo, years ago. Matthew, humbled to silence by this, thanks Farhat penitently, who says **– We still work together eh? This, so whichever new land you go, you have safe place to stand –** Muhammed throws the biggest of parties and for once Matthew sparkles amongst the gathered, the club pumps Arabic hip hop and the boys are down on the dance floor, spinning… Morning comes and Farhat prays that Allah and the Khamsin grant them safe ways to future endeavours in London.

*Sound //*

*Clinking glasses, party, flight airplane to suggest the growth of a business,
success.*

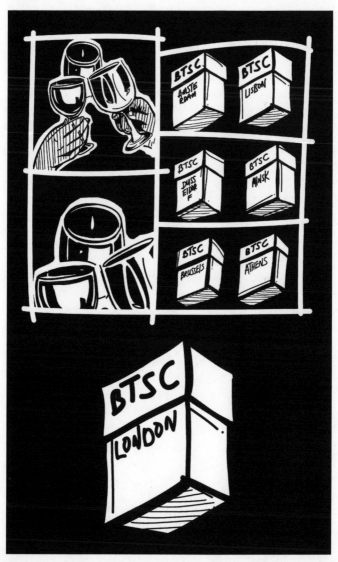

If you had asked the boys of their first impressions, Matthew would have talked of the pace of London, how swift it seemed business happened. Hassan threw them to the swirling madness of gossip columns, model parties, the high-street bloggers all made noise that the Black T-shirt Specialist boys had come. Matthew was shocked to discover kids who'd collected all their shirts...and it seemed cool to be African in London, Matthew asked Hassan who shrugged and replied **– Something to do with liberal guilt and colonial madness; enjoy it! –** If you asked Muhammed his first thoughts, he'd have talked of a night in Soho, the first time he saw two men hug, pull back, kiss each other's eyes, before their lips touched, clutched so tightly as if all the world had paused for them. Muhammed dived into this world as if he had an uncultured tongue and London held the tastes of the planet, he dated like men were going out of fashion. Though they could afford to rent two flats, they chose to share one east of the city and when Muhammed's partners came to visit, Matthew'd suddenly have work to do, retreat to his bedroom, headphones on. Muhammed noticed but never said a word. The first shirt designed in London came from something Muhammed said of a man he'd met in a club **– It's called G-A-Y, met one famous sculptor there, Joseph Plié, two months ago he woke up blind. His birthday is soon, let's do something nice –** Matthew disappeared into his room, next morning stepped out with a slogan-ed shirt of black rubber dots, written in braille: 'We do it best in darkness' it said. Joseph Plié loved it and when news spread, when Josep Plié's followers heard, they ordered five thousand shirts in two days, catapulting Matthew to further fame, Hassan asking from him new shirts, Muhammed saying **– slow down Matthew, there's no rush –**

A bar in Mayfair, one year later. Matthew and Hassan work so tightly, there isn't much for Muhammed to do. Journalists, wanting the quiet artist focus mostly on

Matthew. Muhammed is never asked about shirts. Instead, with deep concern, they'd lean forward and ask **– What's it like to be a gay Muslim –** Muhammed storms out of these interviews, stops attending photo shoots, with nothing left for him to do, he travels by himself **– New frontiers –** he offers if anyone asks and not many do. In trying to find cheaper material, he discovered the darker sides of this business. He has stories of cotton farming in Mali, Australia, Honduras, Uzbekistan, of factory workers; modern day slaves. He'd just returned from South Africa, talking loudly of shirts **– there is an NGO there eh, they gather homeless boys to cut second-hand shirts to pieces, mix the pieces to make new shirts! Then ship them to New York, Toronto, Milan who sell them at astonishing prices! They even sell to Lagos Matthew! They were cutting up our shirts! We have to start a shop back home, I know we can't return, but –** right then a stranger thrusts his arm into Muhammed's sentence, lets it dangle in the air. Their jaws drop, flabbergasted at the man before them. Muhammed, he doubles over laughing hard, gasping for air, Matthew is breathless. Hassan asks **– Who this? You know this man? // Zebra Santana! You bastard man! What are you doing here?! –**

There is a bubble that surrounds old friends. Its sphere is shaded a beige-blue, inside the atmosphere is ticked with in-jokes, old stories, and a guttural kind of laughter that bellies from the deep. A good-natured kind of chaos leaks from where they sit and infects those around them. An older businessman can't help but smile, the manager offers drinks on the house and two ladies listen in to their talk of running under Nigerian heat, torrential rain and childhood play, they bring Hassan up to speed on exactly who Santana is. Santana marvels that his kick to Matthew's chest, started all this, he demands five per cent of their profits, Muhammed traps him in a headlock, grinding knuckles into his skull. The conversation turns serious. Matthew asks **– How are the killings in Jos? –** And Santana's chin drops **– It's getting worse you know. BBC and FOX call it sectarian violence. It is, but it's** deeper than that. It's political, the presidents holiday in Arab countries and the southern Christians don't trust them. Those Christians who studied in Western schools, run businesses in the Muslim north and when Muslim youth leave Islamic schools, they cannot do the jobs. So, the Christians get rich, Muslims, poor. That's why they want Sharia law, to close Western schools, to claim back business and take back their land. It's economic, it is historic, even climate change plays a part; drought messed up all the land, cattle herders can't feed cows. In Jos it becomes tribal because the Berom people own the land, the Fulani people own the cattle. Beroms are Christians, Fulani, Muslims, so they attack houses of worship where they pray for peace, and blood flows throughout our streets. Thousands massacred, more displaced. Thing is, Naija is the America of West Africa, the land of the best and worst; we are influenced by all sorts. When that Danish cartoonist drew Prophet Muhammed, peace be upon him, there were riots, 15 people killed, is that our business? Eh? And that bastard tried to blow up a plane in the States? What kind of madness is that? – Santana looks to the floor visibly frustrated then stares up at Matthew. Muhammed asks the question and Santana confirms their fears – Yes, they burned your house, Halima and Ayah tried to run but they were caught and lashed in public because they didn't know where you were. It wasn't that severe, still, for a thing natural as…you, one lash is a lash too far. Don't look so surprised Muhammed, I don't care if you are gay, I knew before anyway, whenever we tried to toast girls, your mind was never there! – Quiet falls among them now, the bubble of old friends bursts into sharp shards of worry. Matthew was broken by all this, shaken by the news and hearing that Santana knew before him of Muhammed, his face twists to such deeper fury, Santana says – Sorry, I didn't mean to spoil the mood. They're probably alright, I'll check on them for you? I'm going back home, I don't have a job here so… Wait! Wait! I can start your shop!

And this is how Santana joins the Black T-shirt club. He is hopeless; Masters at Oxford, novice at fashion with his trousers too short, his white gym socks and green suede shoes, his shirt tucked in boxers and he thinks it's cool – **Nah –** Matthew says **– this is how we do –** and proceeds to teach him the rudiments of cool: 1) A pair of Converse All Stars and you are good. 2) No tight shirts, always hide your nipples. 3) Try hard to make it look easy. 4) Whatever happens, say no to pink. 5) Sag your trousers, even wearing suits. But all this just leaves Santana confused.

They spend two weeks planning everything: Matthew chooses new designs, Hassan works out the shipping lines, but when it comes to marketing, how to make a splash, Muhammed like a maestro steps into the light, dazzles with his knowledge of exactly what to do: which rapper to speak to, which school is the trendsetter, which magazine, newspaper, newsletter to hit, send samples to that editor, free shirts to which actor big in Nollywood who is making hit after hit, DJs tumble from his tongue tip and Matthew realises Muhammed loved it; the business in Nigeria, he'd controlled it. At the airport, Santana is presented with a gift for Halima and Ayah. He thinks of this carpet, this hand-stitched rug from Cairo...

The very same one Matthew stands on, now, in the living room south of Jos, in Halima's new house, stuck to this spot, the answers to their questions stuffed in the vast gulf between them and him. He scuffs the patterns slightly, shivering, the white box clutched to his chest, uncomfortable under their spotlight stares. He can't remember when last he slept. He has nightmares, loud ones, dark as earth. There are screams, the weight of things pressing down, footsteps, running, metal snapping skin. Even with eyes closed against the patterns, they blaze bright as knives flashing into him; the fractured torment of what came to pass...

Sometimes, there's order to these thoughts. It comes if Matthew thinks with guilt; thinks back to London, imagines the balcony, Muhammed angry. Muhammed

drains the bottle of Champagne and burps into the night.
It is cold. He holds the bottle between his thumb and
forefinger, dangles it over the balcony's edge. London
teems below; its dance of moving cars and human traffic,
like a loose constellation to him. This high up, it is cold.
The bottle slips between his thin fingers, families, couples,
cops pass below, oblivious to the danger he poses above.
Muhammed's caught in the slow-motion fragility of it all,
so, when Matthew calls his name, he startles, the bottle
slips between his thin grip, he tightens just in time. He ties
closed his bathrobe, steps into the room.

Matthew bows low, rising with a flourish, dressed in a grey
pin-stripe suit, cufflinks clink against his glass of Scottish
scotch and Ribena **– Bro, I'm having your favourite,
drink. What'd you think of my bow tie? They're cool
you know, you should watch *Doctor Who* like I've been
telling you to. Aha? Why aren't you dressed? You're
not coming? This is our farewell party Muhammed,
are you still angry about…listen, grow up, 'cause I
don't have time for // You made the choice without
me –** Muhammed speaks in a steel-tipped voice. Matthew
clenches his fist, veins stand out, a thick one throbs his
forehead **–You weren't around, galavanting across the
planet, I made a judgment call, I thought you'd be
happy! I won't apologise, it was the right thing to do
// You made the choice without me –** Matthew looks
to the ground now, his fists limp, the ice cubes wilting in
his drink. They had agreed **– till Santana calls, let's not
take on any new jobs –** Muhammed travelled to some
conference on cotton, Hassan visited, his eyes wide **–
Money in China: silk factory, new kind of fabric, one off**

**shirt // Where?** – Matthew asked **– Guangdong Province, a factory is worked by villagers there –** and Matthew signed the dotted line.

Matthew feels guilt as they pack for China for indefinite a length of time, Hassan waves to them goodbye, Muhammed, a black rock of silence.

*Sound //*

*Flight airplane.*

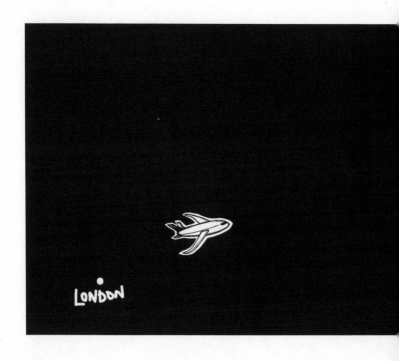

Luo Honshen is 35 and believes in a previous life he'd
made a fine professor. He spent three years in London;
discovered theatre and fashion there before he'd come
home to Zhongshan city. His suits fit well. He strides
with a clipped confidence that hides his lofty thoughts on
Shakespeare and Confucius. He tries to reconcile them as
if lost brothers but Shakespeare is from the gut, Confucius
the head and some things are lost in translation, but his
wife nods, pretends she understands. She loves him, loves
all his achievements including the factory where he works.
Honshen hates the factory he manages but understands
there must be work. For the villagers, it's all they've got
and they know things could be worse. There's a shortage of
jobs, an abundance of people. Don't like the work? Leave,
simple, Honshen thinks as he drives home to his wife and
to his beautiful kids. He stops at the market to buy food he
distributes on Fridays at the factory and buys for his clients,
a box of Guinness, he heard Nigerians liked the drink.

Matthew feels guilt as Muhammed's anger persists
throughout the first week in the City. Avoiding the coldness
of Muhammed's quiet, which deepens or seems to when
he goes near, Matthew hangs out with Luo Honshen,
returns most evenings, late, drunk. Muhammed, furious at
his foster brother, sits by a window, a thick book beside,
awaiting the sun's tireless rise; the cycle to go on. One
evening Matthew comes from a meeting and Mohammed
isn't at home. Not a note in the front room, or a post-it
on the fridge. Matthew worries as darkness swamps the
sky **– Where could he be? He knows no one in China!**
**–** He paces the living room, drags his feet drinking coffee
after pot after mug of mint tea, his guilt chokes him, his
thoughts run wild **– Is he lying in a gutter? Did they rob**
**him? ah! –** At 3 a.m. Matthew is overcome with worry,
Mohammed strides in to his **– Where have you been?!**
**This is not Cairo, London or even Jos, you can't just…**
**you didn't even leave a note, tomorrow we're going**
**to buy mobile phones Muhammed, just look at the**

**time! –** Muhammed laughs, Matthew stops **– I went for a walk OK? –** Matthew nods and Muhammed talks for ten minutes non-stop of all he'd seen. He'd left the city to visit the villages, the broken roads, those who'd tried to rub off his skin, kids who'd asked to touch his hair, their mothers who laughed, starving dogs, the displaced farmers, their reclaimed lands where the government hoped to build new towns. He'd walked out to the vast countryside, where the sky, wide, infinite as ever, humbled his anger at Matthew **– so much money, those kids were hungry // Poverty is poverty, wherever you go –** Matthew says, his voice grey and strained **– Muhammed, sorry I signed the contract without you, it was wrong and // I know –** Muhammed says **– It's OK, just promise it won't happen again.** Muhammed doesn't tell of Wang Bin he'd met in a village, who walked him home, who he'd felt an urgent closeness to, whose smallest brother went up for adoption when their parents couldn't look after them. Wang Bin cried softly as he spoke, his broken English; a noose he struggled through. Mohammed held him close to his chest, Wang Bin lifted up his head, they kissed, hard, on the dirt roads **– I promise –** Matthew says **– it won't happen again –**

Matthew's guilt dims in the weeks after, enough to complete the T-shirt design. Honshen welcomes the work, confides in Matthew something Shakespeare wrote *Neither a borrower nor lender be* and added what Confucius said, how the longest journey starts with one step and Matthew was helping with each shirt to feed the workers, free them of debts. Santana rings, he hasn't found Halima **– but don't worry, I'm getting close –** he says. Muhammed spends time with Wang Bin who works at the factory that makes their shirts. Matthew visited the day before but returned, quiet, worried or something… Muhammed decides to see for himself. So this day after, he goes to the factory, stops at the entrance, shocked at the size. The entire shirt is made here, a heaving tangled production line of a thousand workers, crushed, sweating. Muhammed weaves through looking for Wang Bin.

He walks past bags of silkworms cocooned, here the air
must be moist and warm, so windows are shut, doors
closed. The air is thick with germs and dust. Workers strip
down to their waist for the heat, their skin turns sallow
after months of this. If they finish, they go home, but few
meet the task, so sleep on the floor on the boards laid out.
There are children here, least a hundred of them, scruffy,
eyes inflamed, fingers swollen from dipping bare hands
in vats of boiling water; gathering strands of silk from
cocoons, to feed the machines that spin them to thread.
Now, Muhammed trips over pipes of hot water that fill
open vats, part filled with black dye. Inside, its blades slice
the churning water, they slash the black broth like swords
in moonlight. The steam and chemicals rise through the
air. It's poison and workers wear no masks. Muhammed
covers his nose and runs past to the side where the thread
comes out black. The thread is fed to wooden looms and
the women in them weave in the damp, dim light of the
factory, above, one bulb swings **– the fabric is beautiful**
**–** Muhammed thinks. Wang Bin works where the fabric
is cut. Most crouch, some sit, all waiting their turn. Some
have bandaged hands, some missing fingers, fanning
themselves in the cramped heat. Wang Bin waves excitedly
and breaks Muhammed's heart **– I'm coming –** he says.
He climbs the stairs, crosses the bridge over the open vats,
its blades turning, where Honshen's office and Matthew's
office is. Muhammed wonders where to begin **– he signed**
**this contract, what should I say to him? –** He leans by
the door, scratches his head and the phone in his pocket
starts to ring **– Hello? Hello? –**

Muhammed, he burst into Matthew's office holding his
phone **– Santana's on the line! He's found them –**
Muhammed turns the speaker phone on **– Hello? –** There
is weight in the air, the stillness before rain **– Hello?**
**// Muhammed, where are you? // Mama, I'm fine.**
**// Muhammed, come home, it has been too long**
**// Mama, things aren't…simple // You are my son**
**Muhammed, come home –** Muhammed holds his phone,
and there are tears **– OK, I'll leave tomorrow –** Matthew

turns sharply – // err…there's work to do, we'll come in a week or two. // Matthew, I'm going home // We have to finish the job…er…Mama, Santana, we will call you later? // Matthew don't you dare – Matthew shuts the phone – Muhammed, what's up? Why are you in a rush? Business is going well… // Matthew, look around. Why are we here? Have you seen downstairs? those people, how much is Honshen paying them? How much are the shirts? Did we come to China to exploit these people? // No! Muhammed, we are helping them // This is help? // Yes! The factory almost closed, Honshen said, we're putting food on their tables. You said yourself, families are broken, children sent away // Oh, so it's about you eh? Everybody clap for Matthew Zangho, saviour of China. We have our own problems at home. You know how crazy this business is? Desperate cotton pickers sweating for coins, Americans and their slave trade farms, bribing Brazilians to shut up so they sell cheap product across the world. Second-hand shops that 'collect for charity' and sell Matthew, SELL! in Nairobi, Haiti. Chemicals in the fields that cause cancer; those dark-skinned kids in India paid nothing, nothing, and we are one of them! You can map global poverty down to one shirt, one black T-shirt Matthew. From our stall in Jos to this huge factory, something's wrong, something always goes wrong. This is too big for us Matthew, let's go home. We can control things there, we can do this. // Not with you Muhammed, not with you! They'll kill you // I don't care anymore! I'm tired // Why d'you want to go where you can't be… yourself. London, Milan, San Francisco, you can be who you are there! // I don't know who I am. I'm tired, of ticking boxes, I'm gay, I'm an ex-pat, I'm African, I'm a black African, I'm Hausa, I'm Nigerian O! Muslim, this one, that one…journalists asking stupid questions 'What's it like to be… I DON'T KNOW! I just want to be a man again eh? Where people look like us, talk like us, No labels, no colour, no shirts, nothing. They are waiting for us Matthew… Halima, Ayah, our family. We're connecting death here, one shirt at a time.

**Let's go home brother // I'M NOT YOUR BROTHER!
You ruined my life Muhammed. I wanted to do this
in Naija, build this there, but I have it here, now. I'm
helping, I'm doing something right. I'm helping them,
all those...those men you are fucking! Think I don't
know about Wang Bin, that I don't see you?! 15 years
we grew up together, sharing the same bed, fighting
the same fights, crying together, bleeding and you
kept that away from me? ME! Muhammed, ME! You
still won't talk to me about it. You faggot! Fuck off!
Go back to Naija, I hope they lynch you there, you will
burn in hell fire anyway, go and fuck all of them! I don't
care!**

**Muhammed, sorry. I didn't mean that. I just... I'm...**

Muhammed is pressed flat against the door, as far from
Matthew as he can stand. His hand is to his chest as if
stabbed there. He reaches for the door – **Muhammed
wait, let's talk** – Muhammed leaves the room, crossing
the bridge over the mixing vats, its blades turning,
Matthew runs to him – **slow down** – he shouts, he grabs
Muhammed's hand, who snatches it back, Matthew holds
his shoulder, Muhammed throws his foster brother to the
ground, Matthew grabs his feet. Muhammed loses balance.

When it gets here, Muhammed's falling off into the
churning vat, its blades turning, that cave his skull in, break
through the bone, the black dye mixing with Muhammed's
blood, chewing through limbs, twisting him up. There's
no order, guilt is not enough. Nothing makes sense and
Matthew, he trembles, speechless, in the room. He flinches
in Jos, he shudders in the gloom, he quivers on the carpet,
Halima watching. From afar, he looks like a child who had
lost something old, something deep, a hopelessness grooms
his eyes. Closer, by the light that holds him, his still mouth,
his hunched shoulders, Matthew looks like a man who had
lost everything.

–Tell me how he died – Halima whispers – **WHAT HAPPENED!** – Ayah shouts. Matthew cannot speak. How to begin? What *not* to describe? What might hurt least? – **What's in the box? –** Halima asks **– The first one, the first black shirt // It's true isn't it? You want to close the shop? –** Matthew nods. Ayah stands **– I can't let you, you will not –**

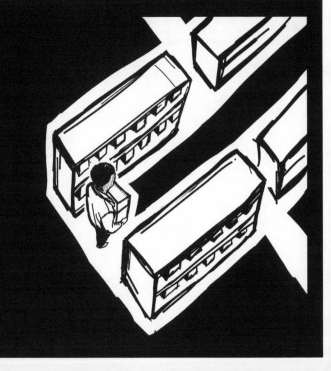

Matthew puts the box in the space he'd left and changes into the first black shirt. He runs his thumb along the print and thinks it funny this started it all. There's dust on his hand and he imagines Cairo, the Khamsin blowing through stalls; Farhat prayed for both their souls. He asked no questions over the phone, just did exactly as Matthew told. Hassan argued and finally stopped **– I'll do it Matthew, but this is wrong –** He made phone calls, cancelled every order, gathered unsold shirts from the world and flew them back to this shop in Jos that Matthew stands in now; the shelves stuffed.

One corner holds the silk from China. Matthew cannot look at them for he knows their dye is mixed with Muhammed's blood. Even with eyes closed against the world, every shade of black reminds him of that blood, every black shirt speaks to him of trust, of love, of sex, of money, of God, of Muhammed's father walking home from work. Matthew was devastated when he heard the story but understood what Halima had done. All this comes with the night that hulks, that swims through the curtain, rooting Matthew to the spot. There are thoughts in his emptiness, thunderous ones, soundlessly, he is strangled in his shirt. The tremendous weight of it all.

Matthew lifts the can of gasoline, pours some onto the last box. Lifts the liquid over his head; he tilts till the fluid begins to fall, pours until, drenched to his core, his skin glistens in the dark of his shop. He casts his eyes over the boxes packed with shirts for one last time, takes out a lighter and holds it, waiting, he waits, as the sirens come.

*Blackout //*

*One stage: performer flicking lighter. Once, twice, third time it comes on.*

*Sound //*

*Fire, burning.*

*End.*